I.B.B.Y launch
31 Merrion Sq. Dublin
20 - 11 - 2002.

A BRIDGE OF CHILDREN'S BOOKS

The Inspiring Autobiography of a
Remarkable Woman

Jella Lepman was the founder of the International Youth Library (IYL) in 1946 and the International Board on Books for Young People (IBBY) in 1952. Born in Stuttgart in 1891, she was the second of three daughters of a Jewish factory owner. She organised an international reading room for children when she was only seventeen. Her husband, a German American, died when her two chidren were tiny, leaving her a widow at thirty-one. She became a journalist and in 1928 published her first children's book. When Hitler came to power, she lost her post in the German Democratic Party and on the advice of friends sought safety in London. This autobiography begins nine years later when she was persuaded to return to post-war Germany.

A Bridge of Children's Books

THE O'BRIEN PRESS
DUBLIN

in association with

IBBY IRELAND and USBBY

This edition first published 2002 by The O'Brien Press Ltd,
20 Victoria Road, Dublin 6, Ireland.
Tel: +353 1 4923333; Fax: +353 1 4922777
E-mail: books@obrien.ie
Website: www.obrien.ie

Published in association with:
IBBY Ireland,
Church of Ireland College of Education, Rathmines, Dublin 6, Ireland
and USBBY,
c/o International Reading Association,
800 Barksdale Road,
PO Box 8139, Newark, Delaware
19714-8139, USA.
E-mail: acutts@reading.org
Website: www.usbby.org

Originally published in Germany as *Die Kinderbuchbrücke*
© 1964 by S Fischer Verlag, Frankfurt am Main,
and republished 1999 by the International Youth Library, Munich.
Translated into English by Edith McCormick.
Translation copyright © 1969 by American Library Association and Brockhampton Press Ltd

ISBN: 0-86278-783-1

British Library Cataloguing-in-Publication Data
Lepman, Jella
A bridge of children's books : the inspiring autobiography of a remarkable woman
1.Lepman, Jella 2.International Youth Library 3.Youth workers - German -
Biography 4.Women educators - Germany - Biography 5.Educators - Germany -
Biography 6.Reconstruction (1939-1951) - Germany
I.Title
943'.0874'092

Editing, layout and design: The O'Brien Press Ltd
Printing: CPD Books

Contents

Thanks

It is a significant act of renewal that this biography is republished with new text and historic illustrations to mark the fiftieth birthday of IBBY. Many people have helped, and they include: in Ireland, IBBY and O'Brien Press colleagues; in the US, Alida Cutts (USBBY) and Joan Irwin (IRA); in Japan, Tayo Shima; in Switzerland, Mary Robinson and the charming and tireless Leena Maissen; in Germany, Dr Barbara Scharioth of IYL, Jella Lepman's daughter Anne Marie Mortara Lepman and her son Guy Lepman, who sadly died on 24 April 2002.

This edition is dedicated to the vision of Jella Lepman and her worldwide IBBY family who make her ideals a continuing reality.

Michael O'Brien, IBBY Ireland

Foreword – Mary Robinson
UN High Commissioner for Human Rights

Jella Lepman is an inspirational figure in the field of human rights – specifically social and cultural rights. She empowered children in one of the most efficient and effective ways, by ensuring they had access to books, in the very difficult context of post-war Germany in the 1940s and 1950s.

For many years, covering the Second World War period, the only reading material most German children had had access to was propaganda of one sort or another. Lepman brought books to these children – books that informed and entertained them and helped enhance their creativity. Hers was a daunting task then – and sadly a challenge that exists today in many parts of our very unequal world.

Jella Lepman researched, cajoled, begged and borrowed from all quarters. She set up travelling exhibitions of books when the population had barely enough to eat. She was inspired in 'knowing that behind me marched invisible throngs of children urging me on'.

Lepman dreamed the impossible, yet worked to make it a reality. Her vision of a library of children's books from all over the world became a wonderful reality. Today, we can all enjoy the unique benefits of the International Youth Library in Munich.

This book also describes her pioneering work in founding IBBY – now spread throughout the world. In my role as UN High Commissioner for Human Rights, I was happy to support IBBY's mission to promote international understanding through children's books. I especially commend IBBY's work in developing countries.

Children's books and the kingdom of the imagination that they represent can be inspirational. I hope that the legacy of Jella Lepman will inspire people to fight racism and xenophobia throughout the world and secure all human rights for all.

June 2002

Introduction — Tayo Shima
President, IBBY

A Bridge of Children's Books is an autobiographical account of the life of IBBY's founder Jella Lepman, originally published six years before her death in 1970. A German journalist, Lepman had sought refuge from the Nazis in Britain. At the end of the Second World War she was requested by the American army to return to Germany to develop cultural and educational projects for women and children.

Back in her devastated native land, Lepman describes how she sought out the German intellectuals who had survived this tragic era in their homeland's history, and the disappointments and aspirations they shared with her. She realized that 'there simply were not enough people who had stood up through the terror of those years.' After what she heard, Lepman resolved to devote herself to the reconstruction of the country. She also observed children struggling to survive in the war-scorched landscape. Listening to their countless tales of the horrors of war, she was astonished to find that their eyes still held the look of children everywhere. She began to think that something had to be done to give back to these children free passage to the world of books, a world where they would find spiritual sustenance as they struggled to regain their humanity. In rebuilding order from chaos, Lepman thought: 'If one is to believe in peaceful coexistence, the first messengers of that peace will be children's books.' She proposed the idea of an international children's book exhibition and set about organising it. This incipient effort eventually paved the way for the founding of both the International Youth Library in Munich and the International Board on Books for Young People in Zurich.

Jella Lepman was born in Stuttgart in 1891, the second of three daughters of a Jewish factory owner. She was educated at a local denominational school and later at a boarding school in Switzerland. When she was seventeen, she set up an international reading room for the children of the foreign workers employed at a tobacco factory.

[5]

Just before the First World War, she married Gustav Lepman, a German-American and manager of a trading company in Stuttgart. She had two children, a girl and a boy, but just after her son was born, her husband died from wounds received in the war, leaving her a widow at the age of 31. In order to raise her two children alone, Lepman took up journalism. In 1928 she published her first book for children, *Der verschlafene Sonntag* (The Sunday Overslept). She played a leadership role in the activities of a women's group of the German Democratic Party in Württemberg. When Hitler came to power, she lost her post, and at the urging of friends, sought refuge in London. The story in this autobiography begins when Lepman returned to her homeland nine years later at the request of the U.S. occupation forces. She was fifty-four.

Today, at this starting point of a new century, nothing seems certain about the future of our world. This book, which recounts how the energies of children contributed to the rehabilitation of a society that had experienced terrible oppression and a devastating war, is a chronicle of human society that can give us hope and inspiration for the challenges we face. Responding to the empathy that one human being feels for another, Lepman knew intuitively what ought to be done and quickly went to work, and those around her found her ideas convincing. Lepman's understanding of, and affinity for, children were pure-hearted, and we can see that she exercised her talents and her sensibilities to the utmost for their sake. The many outstanding figures described in the book – people like Eleanor Roosevelt, Erich Kästner and Theodor Heuss – who extended their support to Lepman on the historical stage of postwar Germany's reconstruction, are a splendid testimony to the chain formed by books as a bridge linking people through the course of human history.

The most formidable obstacles to achieving her goal were not people, but the organizations human beings had created and the bureaucrats who had become the tools of those organizations. She sought to run the International Youth Library by going beyond the framework of libraries as they had been until then to respond to the real needs of children. This institution broke epoch-making

[6]

new ground. It became a 'university for children', holding drama workshops and book discussion groups, teaching foreign languages through reading children's books, presenting puppet plays, showing films, developing an art studio, holding international exhibitions of children's self-portraits, and launching the Young People's United Nations.

Her story of the committed undertakings adults began for children, with all their philosophical, artistic, and political concerns, and the children who eagerly joined them in those endeavours is indeed a moving one. Today, the survival of millions of children all over the world is in the balance, just as it was fifty years ago in the defeated Germany Lepman saw. The task that we at IBBY face today is not fundamentally different from the mission Lepman was inspired to pursue. In these pages we can feel very close to this woman with her extraordinary perceptiveness and empathy for others.

Founded by Jella Lepman fifty years ago under the banner of placing books in the hands of children, IBBY – the International Board on Books for Young People – today has National Sections in over sixty countries. Holding the status of an NGO affiliated with UNESCO and UNICEF, it has grown into a worldwide network linking the world of children's books. The conviction that children's books are the key to peaceful coexistence has spread through countries all over the globe and spawned a growing worldwide network of people working in diverse environments and under very disparate conditions. The globalisation of the world economy today is leaving some regions behind, and poverty and illiteracy are still widespread. Political instability, social unrest and damage to the environment slow development in some parts of the world, while in others ethnic strife and bloodshed continue. With the advent of the electronic age, small screens with their contrived visions of virtual experience invade the brief season of childhood.

Many of us active in IBBY today are members of the generation to whom Jella Lepman first handed books, carrying the flame of her hopes for peace and tolerance in the world. Sustained by the institutions she founded, we continue to expand our global

[7]

associations and network through the agency of books. We are keenly aware that there is no limit or end to our work, which must continue from one generation to the next. We will look to the future with confidence as long as there are people all over the world who, carrying on the ideals and ideas of Jella Lepman, have devoted themselves to linking children and books.

A re-edition of *A Bridge of Children's Books* in the German original – *Kinderbuchbrücke* – was published in 1999 for the fiftieth anniversary of the International Youth Library in Munich. It is our sincere hope that the publication of this new English edition on the occasion of IBBY's fiftieth anniversary Congress in 2002 in Basel, Switzerland – home of the IBBY Secretariat – will help to pass along still further the torch of IBBY's mission. We express our deep appreciation to the O'Brien Press and the Irish Section of IBBY who, together with the United States Section of IBBY and the International Youth Library, have made this publication possible.

i

'And if you were reincarnated, what would you rather be, a man or a woman?'

The person throwing this question at me was a colonel in the American Army of Occupation. His drawl suggested that he came from the South. I was sitting next to him in that diabolical device known as a bucket seat. It was the 29th of October 1945 and our plane, a military transport, was on its way from London to Frankfurt.

A rather unladylike comparison to the bucket seat had just occurred to me when the colonel, silent up until then, made an attempt to start a conversation with his question. I could imagine what he was thinking:

'In God's name, what is a woman doing here? Women in uniform are ridiculous enough as it is. I'd rather see them strolling along the Rue de la Paix in chiffon dresses as they do in Paris – we're flying over it now! Headquarters sometimes sure is daffy.'

Not having the slightest idea at that moment of how to talk to American army colonels on official business, or, if you like, on an official flight, I said simply, 'Assuming that's a purely hypothetical question, I suppose I can answer in the same spirit. Preferably neither. I'd like to be a titmouse or a sunflower or . . .'

The colonel nearly toppled out of his seat. This lyricism was even more than he feared. He stared at me without a word, then said bluntly, 'Just why are you in uniform? What does head-quarters want you to do? Can you tell me?'

'Re-education, colonel,' I said, 'or that's the way they put it. I'm supposed to work with women and children. That's all I know at the moment and, probably, all headquarters at Bad

[9]

Homburg knows, too. Maybe somebody imagined that an under-taking such as this needed the feminine touch.'

The plane went into a kind of loop the loop just then and it was impossible to carry on the conversation. I felt like dying. I had taken off that morning without the famous English breakfast and that alone saved the day for me. The colonel, observing my pallor, quietly pressed a pack of chewing gum into my hand, and this, the universal medicine, really helped. I stuck the chewy stuff between my teeth, feeling pretty much like a post-war soldier already. For the rest of the flight, which lasted a few more hours, I kept my eyes closed.

Something strange happens when you close your eyes this way. Suddenly you are in a totally different world, a place of endless breadth and depth, a kind of Alice-in-Wonderland existence. And there an ultimate and genuine freedom begins, trans-forming prisons into houses with open doors and bucket seats into easy chairs.

In this other world where I no longer felt hampered by a uni-form or a seat belt, where colours were not limited to olive drab or grey, the whole prospect of this new adventure overwhelmed me. A week before I had been sitting in an office of the American Embassy in Grosvenor Square, in London, together with an international team of journalists. We were putting together the first issues of a magazine, *Frau und Welt*, which was to appear subsequently in ten languages throughout Europe. However, while working on it we always had the feeling that we were grop-ing in the dark.

I saw myself sitting at a table with my friend Frances McFad-den of *Harper's Bazaar*, and wondering what really would inter-est people who had survived the hell of the Second World War.

'Certainly not fashion pictures from *Harper's Bazaar*,' Fran-ces said, wrinkling her clever forehead.

'How do you know?' I said. 'Maybe they would. Not to show them patterns for making dresses out of sacking, but simply to prove that such things do still exist.'

'That could be,' Frances said. 'We were in London during the blitz, all right, and that was bad enough. But that was "only" war and not the fiendish thing these people have gone through.'

'Think of the "Woman with the Broom," ' I said. 'That kind of subject would be perfect.'

Anne O'Hare McCormick, in New York, had written an article, later reprinted all over the world, which told of how women in Europe had taken up their brooms to sweep up the debris of the war. We had provided the photograph used to illustrate the piece. And how we got it is a story that deserves to be retold here.

We had received a telegram from the editors of *Life* in New York City telling us that one of their best photographers was arriving in London the next morning to get a picture of the 'Woman with the Broom.'

'Where do we get such a woman?' Frances asked, and racked her brains. 'She must be a specific type – I can visualize her, but I don't know where to find her. Not among *Harper's Bazaar* models, that's for sure.'

A thought shot through my head like lightning – why not my Mrs Grabble, priceless Mrs Grabble without whom I probably would never have got through the war?

'Why not Mrs Grabble?' I said, coming to Frances' rescue. She thought this was a fine idea. 'I'll drive home, tell her, and bring her along in the morning.'

Mrs Grabble was just locking the front door when I got home, almost out of breath. As always her dark brown hat draped with a crown of straw flowers drooped half-way down her neck.

'Please,' I called, 'will you come with me to London tomorrow – my treat.' I knew I could not explain the real purpose. London charwomen are a singular breed; never, voluntarily, would she have allowed herself to be the 'Woman with the Broom.'

'Oh, madam, it's nice of you,' she said, 'but I just can't accept. Anyway, I've never been to London.'

That 'anyway' was a *non sequitur*, and her whole response was fantastic. She lived only a few miles from West London and the

[11]

city proper – it took fifteen minutes by Underground to reach the centre of London.

There was no reason to disbelieve her, however – she could be blunt, but she never lied.

'Well then, it's high time you did get to London,' I said.

She turned up the next morning at eleven on the dot, but I hardly recognized her. I am afraid she had gone to enormous expense, even as far as getting a permanent wave. And instead of the birds' nest arrangement that usually adorned her head, she now wore an elaborate structure of curls. Gone was her blue cotton apron with gay patch pockets; in its place she wore something that could once have been her wedding dress.

I wanted to cry, but did not dare show it. So I explained that to my great sorrow our trip to London would have to be postponed. Since her kindness was as great as her capacity to put up with anything, she began immediately to console *me*.

Fortunately, the *Life* photographer arrived seven hours late – in those days schedules were all too easily disrupted. I promised to do my best the following day. And what do you know – everything went beautifully! The curls had fallen out – it was a real wartime permanent wave. The cotton dress and apron, the hat with straw flowers and birds' nest hair – all were back in place.

I told Mrs Grabble that we had to go to London at once. And, oh, her face, her despair at how her dress would shame me! Quickly I threw on my coat, seized the kitchen broom – a real witch's broom made of straw – and hurried her off to the Underground. Not until we dropped into our seats did she cry out, 'For heaven's sake, madam, what are you doing with the broom? You weren't carrying it through the streets with us, were you?'

'Oh, dear,' I said. 'In the rush I must have grabbed it instead of the umbrella.' We both had a good laugh over it.

Emerging into the daylight of Bond Street, I took Mrs Grabble by the hand because she was so overpowered by this new world. We crossed Mayfair and reached Grosvenor Square and the American Embassy building.

Frances met us and offered Mrs Grabble a 'nice cup of tea.' The man from *Life* came at just the right moment and soon we went downstairs and climbed into one of the Embassy's black Bentleys – I still clutching the broom.

We drove through the West End. Mrs Grabble gazed in utter awe at Westminster and was horrified over the bomb damage. Then St Paul's, and all around it the terrible destruction, but the cathedral towering gloriously above the ruins. Mrs Grabble took St Paul's for a luxurious cinema and clasped her hands in delight. We had some trouble in explaining it to her.

'Mrs Grabble, the American photographer here would like to take some pictures of St Paul's,' I said. 'Now here is where my broom comes in handy.'

Quickly Mrs Grabble snatched her old, trusted friend and soon was shrouded in a cloud of dust. She swept as if her life depended on it, and the photographer took picture after picture. Then we asked Mrs Grabble to pose. She smoothed down her hair and tugged at her apron, her hands trembling. She stood stiff as a child posing for a confirmation picture, and afterwards the *Life* photographer bowed before her as though she were a queen.

This picture hangs in her room, immortalizing one of the unforgettable experiences of her life. But 'Woman with the Broom' went round the world, and Mrs Grabble knows nothing about it to this day.

We loved this work of ours until one day an American army colonel, a university professor in civilian life, knocked on our door and asked me point-blank whether – as soon as arrangements could be made – I would fly to American headquarters in Bad Homburg to become an 'Adviser on the cultural and educational needs of women and children in the American zone.'

The colonel-professor was a kindhearted man, as I later found out, but at that moment he terrified me. I had left Germany during the Hitler régime – words are inadequate to describe what that meant. And what had happened since cried out to heaven – oh . . . suddenly my hands flew to my face.

[13]

Men generally, not excepting American colonels, have little patience with women who weep. Tears are weapons they simply are not used to fighting against. I pulled myself together, looked at him, and said, 'Let me think it over, please, colonel. It's not going to be an easy decision to make.'

For two weeks I went through agonies over the question, and nobody could help me. It would have to be a completely personal decision whose fateful consequences I sensed, even though I shrugged them away.

'I envy you,' Frances said. 'You have the education, you know the language, and you've lived with those people. I, now, could never fill such a post. I'd be utterly foreign in it.'

Another friend, the daughter of Sigmund Freud, advised me, 'Don't go. You've already suffered too much. At last you're beginning to put down roots and, anyway, you know people can't be re-educated.'

'Don't go,' others also said. 'Do you believe the Nazi spirit is really dead? It will last for generations, even with the best help in the world. German bombs might have killed you at any time in the last six years. Isn't that enough for you?'

But my situation was more complicated than they imagined. Had only adults been involved, I would not have hesitated to say no. The word 'Re-education' rang hollow in my ears, too, as far as adults were concerned. But children — did that not change matters?

I found it easy to believe that the children all too soon would fall into the wrong hands if no help came from the world outside. Were not Germany's children just as innocent as children all over the world, helpless victims of monstrous events?

At the same time, a picture engraved deep in my memory rose to mind. Shortly before the outbreak of the war I had succeeded, with the help of an English relief organization, in getting the child of a close friend out of Germany. I got word that the train would arrive around midday and the little girl would be met by the family from Leeds who were going to give her a home.

[14]

So I waited, hugging a box of sweets and a warm shawl close to my chest, and peered out into the station concourse, dark and muggy although it was only noon. Homeless myself and in no position to give the child shelter, I stood there lost in thought. Then the children came into view – about fifty of them, boys and girls, mostly between eight and ten years old, all very well-behaved and looking very tired. They wore warm coats and caps and I could picture the mothers, their hands trembling all the while as they bundled up their children.

The serious young faces of these children were a moving sight, for I lived in a country where children still laughed and were full of fun. But these children – what had their eyes seen, their ears heard? And what a parting lay behind them!

I took my little girl in my arms. She hardly said a word. With a placid surrender whose deepest cause I could only guess at, she let herself be led to a table, accepted a bowl of soup, but left untouched an orange that had been put before her, although, for her kind in Germany, oranges no longer existed.

The names of the children were called out, and the people who came for them took the little refugees gently by the hand and one by one led them away. Here and there a woman could be seen kissing and hugging a child in an overwhelming surge of sympathy. It was a remarkable show of love for one's fellows that was taking place here in the waiting-room of a great city's railway station. And, at the same time, what an indictment against those who had consigned these children to such a fate.

More and more clearly, I came to realize that I must not look backward, but to the future, and that I must begin with the children. I could hardly doubt the soundness of this thinking. What right did I have to say no? So I said yes – a provisional yes, perhaps, leaving the door to the old life still open to me.

I shook off these memories and returned to the reality of my flight to Frankfurt. Here I was, now in a uniform and all that went with it. Only those in uniform were admitted to American Headquarters; a special outfit had been created for civilians.

I, too, would much rather have been walking in chiffon down the Rue de la Paix. . .

At about four o'clock in the afternoon we landed at Frankfurt's military airport. We climbed out of the plane and down the steep steps in silence. Once again I set foot on German soil.

A young Canadian secretary and I were the only ones on board who were bound for the Bad Homburg headquarters. A military jeep was supposed to meet us, but none was in sight. So we sat on a bench and basked in the last rays of the October sun. While waiting, we watched a girl in a small rotunda of the temporary reception building as she gave out information, spoke on the phone, and, above all, flirted for all she was worth. It all was a little like watching a film.

This girl was the first German we met. She was pretty, spoke a GI brand of English with absolute ease, had a permanent wave, and wore nylons. The Canadian and I exchanged bewildered glances. Obviously, we both had a misconceived picture in our heads of sackcloth and ashes. We couldn't know that this girl was especially chosen to assist the American army – nor that, while this army forbade GIs to fraternize with the 'enemy', nylons could always be smuggled into a girl's hand. Already we were beginning to realize that we were greenhorns and in for a good many shocks.

After the girl had made several phone calls, a big car finally pulled up instead of a jeep. 'Hello, girls!' the driver said, and we sank into soft cushions no doubt usually reserved for a three-star general.

But even observing Frankfurt from the car we were struck by the big pile of ruins it was. It depressed us so much we began to tremble.

'That's the way it is,' the Canadian said. 'Ghastly, ghastly.' Then she pulled her cap over her eyes and sat without moving for the rest of the ride. It was more than she could take and, in spite of London, I felt much the same way.

I had known Frankfurt as an elegant city of commerce, had,

[16]

as a child, walked along the Main River quay, and in Goethe's house had caught a glimpse into the life of the greatest German of all. All that remained were ruins, rubble, and a grey fog of dust lying over the city like a cloud.

Where were the people? Strangely wary, they crept through the streets. Nothing about them resembled the girl in the airport rotunda. Often it was impossible to tell whether the figure who turned a corner and gathered a bundle of wood from the ruins, with a timid look around, was a man or a woman. They paid us no attention at all, except once when a child waved. She was sitting on a stairway that was half bombed out and in her hand – wonder of wonders – she held an autumn flower. Often since then I have thought of that child.

It was dark by the time we reached Bad Homburg, which at the time was the American Headquarter's base. Guards stood at a gate surrounded by barbed wire and let us pass only after checking our papers carefully. Then lights streamed from all the buildings, the sound of music was borne to us by the wind. People in uniform strolled, laughing, along the residential streets – it was a world completely transformed.

The car lurched to a stop in front of a house marked 'Quartermaster.' Again we had to show our papers, and while my companion was directed to another office, the quartermaster peered at my 'military orders,' first in surprise, then in visible irritation. He shook his head, resolutely grabbed a phone beside him, and a conversation followed, which, understandably, I heard only one side of.

'Colonel, what should I do? There is a *female* here, with the ranking of a major. Where am I supposed to put her up tonight?'

My heart thudded. I was so inexperienced in military matters that I had not even taken the trouble to study my papers. I was, so-called, a major. I had worked my way up phenomenally – on paper.

The quartermaster replaced the receiver, pulled out a drawer behind his desk, and handed me two brown woollen blankets.

'House No. 7, first room on the right. That's all until tomorrow.'

I obediently followed his orders and five minutes later I was standing in an empty room lit by a bulb dangling from the ceiling. We stared at one another, the room and I. Soon there was a knock and my Canadian friend stood in the doorway.

'Ghastly, ghastly,' she said as before. 'But now I suppose we have to find something to eat.'

We followed a stream of headquarters' people towards a brightly lit building at the end of the street. Almost blinded by the light, we found ourselves in a vast dining hall whose tables were laden as for a feast. Soon an American captain walked up and took us each by the arm. 'Can I buy you a dinner, girls?' he said. It was obvious that he was trying to help us over the awkwardness of this first evening, but the question struck me as awfully strange. The expression he used was not to be found in my dictionary of Oxford English. Only gradually did I begin to grasp the mysteries of American slang. For really, his invitation was only the expression of the warmheartedness and helpfulness that is so characteristic of Americans.

I do not remember much more about that evening. The day's events had been too exhausting, and the wonderful security of this American officers' mess enveloped us like an eiderdown. I am afraid that our charming captain did not get his money's worth with the pretty Canadian or with me. We sampled a bit of food and drank a glass of French wine, but it seemed that everything going on around us was like happenings on a stage. I was glad when I got back to my barren but centrally-heated room. There I wrapped two army blankets around me and settled down on the floor. The wool prickled and made my skin itch; it felt like lying on the orthopaedic bed of my girlhood. But soon I fell into a dreamless sleep.

It would be a sin of omission not to mention my first breakfast at American Headquarters. At exactly seven o'clock the doors to the officers' mess were closed; you had to crawl out from under the covers in good time, for the bathroom had to be shared with

[18]

seven others. You joined that community without ceremony. One person would sit in the bathtub while two others scrubbed themselves at the double sink. It was all accepted with colossal matter-of-factness. Even background music was provided by somebody's radio. Since the whole house was for women exclusively, there could be no objections.

The struggle with the uniform came next – knotting the tie – and then galloping off to breakfast in the officers' mess. A sergeant sat at a table by the door. He had to be paid his tokens in the special paper currency issued to the American Army. The charge was ridiculously small. In return we got undreamed-of luxury.

The colonel who had recruited me in London came up to me at once and dragged me off to his table. The place was alive with decorated shoulders, from generals down, including many 'army civilians'. The seating arrangements were thoroughly democratic, and differences in rank did not exist at all.

Waiters and waitresses flew back and forth, all of them so-called 'displaced persons.' They spoke Czech, Polish, Ukranian, always with a few scraps of American thrown in, too. They offered us oatmeal with cream, cornflakes or Rice Crispies, California sugar plums, pancakes with maple syrup, ham and eggs – one, two, or three fried eggs – grapefruit with a maraschino cherry in the centre, toast, fresh-baked rolls or croissants, dishes of jam, and coffee that would have raised the dead.

From all sides good things were pushed towards me. All I had to do was reach out and help myself. Then a curious thing happened – I just could not do it. My stomach still was used to an English 'austerity' diet. It was not only my stomach. I could not help but think of those evacuated children in London, and the little girl on the way to headquarters. So I drank two cups of coffee, ate a slice of toast, but somehow it stuck in my throat, although I knew this was irrational. Why should not the Americans, who had played such a decisive role in defeating Hitler, eat breakfast in their own style? Already they had started a great

[19]

'War Against Hunger' in the occupied zones, but my sense of discomfort got the best of me.

It disappeared later when I sat in the Colonel's spartan office along with his Information Control staff. Briefly he outlined the enormous job ahead of us, first of all, as far as possible separating the wheat from the chaff. Then, with the help of competent and well-intentioned Germans (he had no doubt that such existed) we were to draw up and carry out a programme of cultural reconstruction in the American zone. My job would be to investigate the position of women and children and make suggestions about the form such aid would take.

At first I tried to learn as much as I could from the experiences of others at headquarters who had been appointed to similar jobs, but in different sectors. I soon realized that they, too, were more or less groping in the dark. No one had any precedents to follow. This was a situation unique in history, with the victors assuming that it was their duty to help the vanquished get back on their feet, and puzzled over how to do it.

Later these lofty impulses often were shunted over to the political and economic sphere and branded as mere expediency. Certainly expediency did play a part, but in those days it was only negligible. War, victory, and defeat are concepts painful to the American mind.

At this time an almost missionary zeal prevailed at American Headquarters to bring order out of chaos on a sweeping scale – order cut to the American mould, of course. Such an attitude assumed the superiority of one's own goals and one's own land, and these Americans were not lacking in that. They were sure that their way of life was the one most worth aspiring for. Any doubt, however cautiously expressed, would arouse amazement, if not downright sadness.

I soon realized that I was not going to get a true picture from the green desk at Headquarters. So, whipping up my courage, I knocked on the general's door – one could do that kind of thing at American Headquarters – and presented my case.

General McClure, who commanded the Information Control division, proved that he had a remarkably open mind. There was no trace of military arrogance. Instead, he showed intelligence, sympathy, and action. He agreed to clear the way at once for me to make a fact-finding trip that would last several weeks. One week later I set out on my journey.

This is when I encountered my first jeep – then as now an incomparable and ingenious vehicle, although in no sense was it made for female army civilians. The running boards were so high that you either had to have the driver pull you up or get him to give you a boost from behind. Most of the jeeps were war veterans crowned with glory, if a jeep can be so described. The seats were hard and you were bounced up and down, but you soon got used to that, and there were plenty of army blankets to go round.

I never can think of the jeep except as a living creature related to the horse, or at times the camel – in any case, invested with peculiarities all its own. What a sense of freedom seized one when once you were up in the saddle! Wind and snow might blow about you, the summer sun might burn your neck, but at least you were not riding round the countryside in a glass box – you became part of the surroundings yourself. And how rarely did a jeep conk out. Imperturbably it flew over bomb holes and craters, a trustworthy magical steed!

On the way to Heidelberg I saw the first *autobahn*, famous as the 'unrivalled accomplishment of the Hitler régime.' And it was impressive, even when full of bomb holes, though at the time it struck me as a sort of surgical incision through the countryside.

My driver, Joe, was a young American from the hinterlands. He had never left his little midwestern town until the Army shipped him overseas for the invasion. Europe was a completely unfamiliar part of the globe to him, and he drove about it in his jeep as if he were on Mars. Seldom did he check the swear words which, luckily, I rarely understood.

From time to time I would show him on the map the place we would be aiming for. At first I suspected that he was illiterate, but that was out of the question in the American Army. He wasn't far from it, though. Soon, however, I grew to have a real affection for him and his view of life. Gradually I got to know members of his family from photographs and from comments he made. I knew he had a fiancée waiting for him, and like a child before Christmas he drew red lines through the squares on the calendar to cross off the days before his discharge.

He kept his jeep well in hand. He was not the most skilful driver, but he was a safe one. The only thing that time and again had me worried was his sense of direction. I do not think he had even mastered the cardinal points of the compass, at least he would always look at mine askance. Sometimes he argued with it as if it were a human being. 'How'd it know where the sun goes down?'

Heidelberg was the first place we stopped. It was the least damaged of all German cities and overflowing with refugees. Around noon our jeep pulled up in front of Professor Alfred Weber's house. A woman opened the door and told me that the professor now lived upstairs in the attic.

I climbed the stairs through the autumnal gloom and Professor Weber appeared in a doorway. We stood looking at each other as if we were seeing ghosts. He was emaciated down to the bone and had gone completely grey. His face was so pale it was almost translucent. I offered him my hand but he shrank back from grasping it.

'No, I cannot take your hand,' he said. 'Germany has brought too much horror and misery upon the world, and I too am guilty.' His hands were shaking and there was nothing I could do but take him by the arm into his study. His writing desk stood against the slope of the attic ceiling. It was bitterly cold, and the wind blew through windows that had been pasted up with paper.

An unforgettable conversation finally reunited us. Here was one of the most distinguished scholars in Germany – indeed, in all of Europe – who, as a sociologist and political scientist, has uttered many brave words of warning to the world. Never had he yielded in any way to the 'system'. You could see in his face how greatly he had suffered. Yet he was ready and willing to take the guilt of others upon himself.

He held his head in his hands as tears rolled down from his eyes. 'I have just written to General de Gaulle,' he told me. 'The division of Germany is a disaster. It will have the gravest political consequences. All I can do is send him a warning.'

His hopelessness shocked me. He looked with anxiety on the coming winter and the misery of the homeless. Above all, he did not believe that Germany could muster the spiritual strength to control her destiny. He did not know then that his pessimism was groundless in many respects, though, unfortunately, not in all.

An hour later I spoke to Professor Willy Hellpach, a noted physician, psychologist, journalist, and once Democratic candidate for the presidency of the Reich. He had a totally different attitude. Hardly a word was spoken about the past, though he too condemned it severely. His thoughts were all directed towards the future. He was deeply disappointed at the meddling of the Americans whose plans, like skyscrapers, always went one better than his own. He was terrified too of their scanty knowledge of the country they now 'ruled.' 'At least the English and French are Europeans and possess certain facts by virtue of their birth.'

His prophecy for the future (I jotted it down verbatim in my notebook) was this: 'The real dispute in the world is just beginning now. If the western powers don't oppose communism with bold and creative ideas of their own, in a generation or two the world will be communist.'

There followed a brief respite with the widow of Max Weber, Dr Marianne Weber, one of the most intelligent and influential campaigners in the fight for women's rights. The refinement and sensitivity showing in her beautiful features made her look as though she already belonged to a different world. We sat chilled to the bone on a sofa in her icy reception room, which now served as her living-room and bedroom as well. The intellectual *élite* of Heidelberg had once used this as a meeting place on Sunday afternoons. Now this house on a hill along the Neckar was swarming with refugees who had no idea under whose roof they lived. Their laundry was strung out on twine through the corridors, worn and tattered.

Before going on, I phoned headquarters and asked the captain responsible to get some packages of food to these half-starved creatures. Not one of them had even mentioned the word 'hunger.'

So that was Heidelberg, the city least damaged by the war! I had no illusions about what was to come. Soon our jeep was bumping along over frozen roads through one of the most beautiful regions of southern Germany, but, naturally, in the wrong direction. Vainly I suggested to Joe that he use the Neckar as a guide, but all he did was shake his head. 'Never heard of Neckar.' We must have had a third, invisible companion in our jeep through that whole adventurous trip – a guardian angel. He had his work cut out for him as we clattered along over the many unexploded bombs.

By evening, Stuttgart lay below us in a valley where only a few lights showed. Joe, I am glad to say, had no idea that I knew Stuttgart. He sat stolidly in the driver's seat like a stuffed bird, and, working the chewing gum that had stuck to his teeth, muttered, 'What a hole!' And I could hardly blame him. We had pulled up in front of one of the few sturdy buildings left in the inner city, the *Tageblatt* tower. Joe had found his way there by asking a military policemen how to get to the offices of the military government. This building was the publishing house where I had once worked. 'The wheel has turned full circle,' a voice inside me said. I was trembling as I climbed out of the jeep.

A *Life* reporter happened to be standing there when the porter ran out of his cubicle and started waving wildly.

'You're back again. Wonderful! Now everything will be all right.'

It was an astonishing performance, considering that this man had sat in this same cubicle for the last twelve years, greeting everybody who entered with a rousing 'Heil Hitler!'

Within five minutes the compositors and printers were hurrying up to me, a surprising number of them from the old crew. Whatever they themselves believed, they had first worked for the democratic newspaper, then for the Nazi paper, and now they had offered their services to the paper licensed by the Americans.

The greetings tumbled over one another in a rush, while the *Life* reporter pushed eagerly in among the crowd. Their refrains were always the same: 'The spectres are gone. Now everything will be all right again.' It was that easy — yesterday was yesterday, today was today. It took my breath away. Not only was I shocked at witnessing how one of the most horrifying catastrophes in world history was dismissed, but how it had been passed over so matter-of-factly.

I felt like a stranger surrounded by strangers. Yet it was not hate that moved me, but compassion. And not compassion for these people as individuals, they only partly deserved it. But for the limits of human nature in general that permitted these attitudes to exist. A hurricane had devastated the land, millions had been killed, millions more had lost their homes, the boundaries of nations had collapsed, cities had gone up in flames, let alone culture and civilization, which had turned into exceedingly questional concepts. And all the survivors wanted for themselves was for everything to be the same as it was before!

I took a strong dose of sleeping pills and was still feeling groggy the next morning when there was a knock on the door. The next thing I knew Elly Heuss-Knapp stood before me. She was the wife of Theodor Heuss, then minister of culture for Württemberg and later president of the Federal Republic. No words were necessary. No matter how long we had been separated, we still lived in the same world.

We carried on a long conversation about the kind of help women and children would need. Elly Heuss, like Marianne Weber, thought that soup kitchens and CARE parcels were very wonderful and necessary, but 'spiritual nourishment' and all that those words imply was of even greater importance. Here and there we could detect the first faint stirrings in that direction, but no one had formed a clear picture yet – and that was what was needed. People were either ardently pro-American or the reverse, both were bad. And the disease of Nazism – who could expect it to be otherwise? – was far from dead. There simply were not enough people who had stood up through the terror of those years and who now could take over leadership.

I can still see the face of Elly Heuss before me, worn with suffering, her shoulders always hunched up as if she were under a cold shower. She had managed to care for her family by doing advertising work for chemical companies, and countless times had despaired of her husband's life, which often had been in grave danger. She held few illusions, but had a great store of courage.

I later also met Theodor Heuss, in one of the hillside villas that had been turned into a ministry. His hair was white, his body showing the effects of hunger, but I could sense the crackling energy emanating from him. We spoke very little about ourselves and our own experiences, but a great deal about the fortunes of those who had died.

Theodor Heuss shared my worry over those now assuming leadership in Germany, those without political taint. Would they develop fast enough to meet the demands of their difficult task? Many of them lacked the professional training and experience that would be needed, particularly in the fields of publishing and education.

'As an educational authority,' Heuss said, 'a military government is always bound to be a dubious proposition.' There was no denying that he was right.

I also spoke with Reinhold Maier, once chairman of the Swabian democratic party and now president-minister of Württemberg. Being a typically obstinate Swabian, he had fought his private war against Hitler. His wife and children were still exiled in England, but were soon going to rejoin him.

My friend, Konrad Wittwer, bookseller and Württemberg's

state secretary, spoke with urgency about the people's hunger for books, especially books that were from the free world and banned to them for twelve years.

'And children's books?' I asked.

'Children's books? Oh, there aren't any of those left whatever. Those are more needed than all the others.'

ii

I rode on through postwar Germany, talking to university professors, educators and publishers, and living experiences often so starkly in contrast to the other, that sometimes I would sit beside my driver, Joe, in a state of total collapse. Without a word he would hand me his flask of whisky.

Black was not black, white not white. There were numberless and unimagined shades in between. One person had been a member of the party precisely so that he could use the security position afforded him to help the oppressed. Another had never carried a party card, but still assumed the burden of guilt. There were millions of fellow-travellers, and it was difficult to explain to them that you cannot be a sympathizer without bearing equal responsibility for the régime.

One time I sat in the apartment of a doctor who had saved his hospital by entering the party. He despised the Nazis, his wife was a Swede, and the entire family was very musical. He sat down at the organ to play a Bach fugue, and in the middle of a *cantabile* he suddenly broke off, shook his head, and murmured to himself, 'Do I still have a right to play this music . . .?'

Another time I met the wife of a Jewish lawyer. He was dead, but by some strange act of grace she herself had been saved from Theresienstadt. Though a sensitive and cultured human being, now when she rode in crowded streetcars she would force other passengers to give up their seats to her. 'I was in a concentration camp,' she would say. 'I have more rights than all of you.' From Theresienstadt she had automatically been returned to Germany because once she had lived there. Now she knew just a single wish – to leave again as soon as she could. Never had I seen human features which expressed such restlessness.

Also unforgettable was my visit to an old children's nurse. In the same room where the people she once worked for had entertained guests, she now kept her bed. The entire family had been taken away within an hour, leaving the nurse behind to care for the house.

She lay there, half crippled, and beside her sat her sister, who still bore the unmistakable signs of a Nazi fanatic. She didn't try to hide it either, and I shouldn't have let her remark bother me. 'It's a good thing the Jews left in time to be spared the bombs that came down on the German cities,' she said. 'No one ever bombed Theresienstadt or Auschwitz. People must never forget that.'

The jeep rattled on over the badly pocked roads. Joe was suffering agonies of homesickness. The Middle West and his small town seemed more like paradise every day. Here one PX was like another, and the winter-swept, ravaged land stared back at him with hostility. The language was full of alien sounds. 'I wish I'd never seen this d— Germany,' he said. 'I want to go home. I want to go home.'

Poor Joe, he had no idea of how many people envied him his warm U.S. Army uniform, his PX card, and all the splendid things he could get with it. He was an American, a legendary being to whom girls waved along the street. But he wanted nothing to do with them. 'Can't talk to them,' he said. 'You can't make love if you can't talk. No, no . . .'

More and more my attention was being drawn to the children. They clung to our jeep in clusters wherever we stopped. Their thin, half-savage faces showed their hunger. They snatched at everything we offered them. They even babbled in American-style English, but it was easy enough to understand them without words.

I talked to them, asked about their mothers and fathers, their homes. I got the same answer each time. 'No home . . . don't know where mother and father are. On the road . . . somewhere on the road. Or dead, dead . . .'

And the stories they told, matter-of-factly and without emotion;

[29]

the experiences they described – hangings, shootings, murder, robbery, crimes of the basest kind. Nothing had been kept from them. In spite of everything their eyes still were the eyes of children, and that was the astonishing thing. Scarcely comprehensible.

Many of them banded together in bombed buildings, air raid shelters, under stairways, even in caves in the woods. They were thrown completely on their own wits. It was necessity that forced them to bunch together into gangs. I noticed once a girl about six, a graceful little thing who even in her ragged clothing was something to behold. Clusters of curls fell on her shoulders, her violet eyes gazed out at the world in innocent wonder.

Either this child stood quietly, in an appealing pose, waiting for something to be given to her, or she approached the American officers whose PX was nearby, extended her little arms to them, and said 'Please' in a drawn-out plea. So many gifts were showered on the little beggar that she had to spread her apron to receive them all. She curtsied, then vanished down a side street.

Following, I saw her disappear into a building entrance. Cautiously I peered inside. I saw two big toughs with gross features standing there, emptying the contents of the girl's apron into a large travelling bag. This was done quickly, and then the thugs ran out a back door, leaving the little girl alone and empty-handed. Tears ran down her cheeks. I approached her quietly and took her hand.

'Can I do anything for you?' I asked.

All the disappointment and childishness disappeared instantly from her face. She looked at me with suspicion, wrenched herself free, and was gone as though swallowed by the earth.

Speaking once to a social worker about this incident, I was told that it was part of everyday life. These little waifs received a thorough training for their jobs, and at the same time were so terrified of their ringleaders that they never thought of betraying them. The goods were sold to dealers on the black market, and at the end of the day the little decoy would receive some trifling payment. She had to make the best of it, since she didn't want to be expelled from the gang.

Other children, themselves needing care, assumed the duties of the head of the family. A train of younger brothers and sisters depended on them. It was astonishing how well they coped with their difficult jobs. Here were these diminutive creatures scouring the ruins for wood, carrying loads, rummaging through rubbish, running errands, and selling part of their ration coupons on the black market. Girls not yet eight years old put heart and soul into washing and brushing their smaller brothers and sisters, and they portioned out whatever grubby fare they were able to cook from meagre provisions. Their efficiency and ingenuity had to be admired.

Nevertheless, I could not forget the millions of children who were small shadowy figures behind these others. The thought of them tormented me night after sleepless night. Hadn't they been torn from their mothers and fathers, or shut up with them in camps unfit for human beings? Hadn't they been humiliated, tortured, beaten, starved, finally to end up in the gas chamber? Compared with them, even these children of the ruins were lucky.

Not even the worst November and December storms could daunt the jeep. As he pulled up patiently before numerous military offices, ministries, newspaper buildings, and radio shacks, Joe would warm his hands over one of those stoves with the pipe sticking up in the air. On my part, I had to give 'advice' for the first women's newspapers, women's pages in dailies, women's broadcasts. And each time a veritable wall had to be scaled. What a change when I was able to speak with publishers about bringing out children's books! Here was *my* element.

Most publishers suggested beginning with *Robinson Crusoe, Gulliver's Travels, Uncle Tom's Cabin.* I found it hard to restrain my laughter. This, obviously, was less a matter of interest on their parts for the classics of children's literature than it was interest in the literature of the occupying powers, which would demonstrate the sincerity of their anti-Nazi spirit and their broad-mindedness. And what of their own children's classics? More, what about the modern children's literature of other countries? We would have to find a way to inform editors about foreign books for children. This would have to be one of my first ventures.

Thus, for the time being it seemed that I could call my fact-finding mission to a halt. I didn't know whether I had really gained an insight into the exceedingly complex conditions of post-war Germany's women and children. That would have to be demonstrated.

'Let's go home,' I said to Joe.

'To England or the States?' he said, his eyes twinkling. Then he gave spurs to his mount and it practically galloped by itself back to its stall. I jolted up and down in my seat and every bone in my body ached. But that didn't seem to matter any more.

'A soldier's life is a hard one,' Joe said, and in his tone there was a note of sadistic pleasure at my discomfort. After all, women didn't have to put on a uniform and chase around the world in jeeps.

Once a week at Bad Homburg headquarters, a 'general' meeting would be held where the heads of various sections gathered under the chairmanship of General McClure. Among a dozen high-ranking officers I sat, the lone woman, to give my report on the fact-finding expedition.

I didn't feel a trace of soldierly courage. On the contrary, my heart beat wildly. I had no idea of what people meant by military regulations. I didn't even know the correct form for addressing an officer.

So first I briefly stated that in so far as women and children could even be placed into a single category, nowhere had their lives taken on any distinct shape. Those who had escaped Hitler's lunacy still were existing in a no-man's land, though the spirit they showed certainly made you sit up and take notice. These people had taken a beating, but by no means were they beaten.

They had to be given 'something strong to hold on to' – a fact that their fellow countryman, Humboldt, had known.

One principal measure of achieving this, I suggested, would be an exhibition of the best children's books from various nations. 'Bit by bit,' I said, 'let us set this upside down world right again by starting with the children. They will show the grown-ups the way to go.'

The generals, colonels, and majors listened politely, if with some surprise. Occasionally a star-studded shoulder shrugged, unconsciously, but unmistakably. Then the general climbed to his feet, and something in his voice intimated that he was interested in the plan. First, of course, he asked the sobering question, 'Where will the Information Control division get the money to fund such a travelling exhibition? The budget provides nothing for children's books.'

Here I leaped my first hurdle.

'General, if I may ask, why did headquarters take on an adviser for women's and youth affairs if there were no means to implement the position?'

A smile played at the corners of the general's mouth, and even the others looked amused.

'That's not a bad point,' he said. 'But unexpected demands are being put on the army by postwar conditions. Right at this moment I don't know where we could find the money for your plan, which strikes me as an excellent one. I'll send a memo to Washington.'

I knew by now what a memo to Washington meant – at the least, a few months delay. I could imagine the requests for further information, replies sent back again, and the pages of the calendar I would be tearing off before any 'action' could be taken. Meantime, Germany's children would have to do without books unless somebody pulled out the old Nazi versions, while the number of *Robinson Crusoe* publishers would reach staggering proportions.

But there was no turning back now – I had already gone full sail

[33]

into the open sea. If nobody would help me, then I would have to help myself. I'd had lots of practice in that.

So I tried to make a provisional arrangement.

'May I have your permission – I'm afraid my terminology isn't very military – to get the books without any money? Meanwhile, my proposal for the international children's book exhibition can make its own way through the Pentagon. I'm sure we'll be able to use whatever money will be authorized.'

Who spread the word that American army officers have shields of armour over their hearts? Anybody could feel the barometer climb and the atmosphere grow noticeably warmer.

'Excellent!' the general said. 'However, I must bring up one question. Six months ago most of the countries you intend to appeal to for books were at war with Germany. They might not be too receptive to the idea. Do you actually think people are going to send you crates of books willingly?'

Was this doubt justified? A voice cried out in me, 'No!'

'If the war really is over,' I said, 'if one is to believe in peaceful coexistence, the first messengers of that peace will be these children's books. Help me with this experiment. I promise you, you'll never regret it.'

The general hesitated no longer. 'All right,' he said. 'Even if we can't support the project financially to begin with, we'll back it another way. This venture called the International Exhibition of Children's Books wins first priority. I'll send you authorization in writing to get your project off the ground.'

Had it been possible to throw one's arms around a general during a meeting of the big brass, I would have done so. I left the conference with wings on my heels – in my clumsy, rubber-soled army shoes. The talking was over. At last we could begin working on a practical solution.

Anybody who pictures the U.S. army headquarters, then housed in the building which used to contain the German ministry of revenue, as an old, imposing residence filled with easy chairs,

[34]

is mistaken. The building was comparatively new, a staid structure taken over, apparently, without furnishings. The American Army had fitted it out with mass-produced pieces of furniture set against the bare walls, harsh and shiny. If you so much as borrowed a chair from a neighbour you committed a serious offence, because every object was carefully inventoried and had to stay where it was placed. This regulation was watched over with the hundred eyes of Argus. 'Orderlies' even served as lookouts, most likely.

Typewriters were especially sacred, and only after working hours did you dare lay hands on one. Then as soon as you began softly typing away on the keys, a patrolling soldier would appear, making his regular rounds through the building, and you would have to explain to him why you were sitting at the machine after hours.

I am not a very good liar, but I'm afraid that at this period I began paving my way to hell. I always mumbled the name of some high-ranking officer whose work I was being forced to slave over every night. If I had admitted I was typing requests for children's books from foreign countries, probably I would have been arrested for fraud.

There I sat, not a soul in sight, setting something into motion that later proved to be quite an important undertaking. Luckily, I had friends and colleagues to turn to in the profession, especially the American diplomatic representatives. With my 'first priority' in hand, I asked them for advice and assistance in forwarding our requests to the right places.

I no longer have a copy of the letter I sent out at that time. It probably is buried in some file in Washington. However, I still remember how it would have read:

'Dear Sir:

'This letter contains an unusual request. May we ask for your most special understanding?

'We are searching for ways to acquaint the children of Germany with children's books from all nations. German children are practically without any books at all, once their literature from the Nazi period has been removed from circulation. Also, educators and publishers need books from the free world to orient and guide them. These children carry no responsibility for this war, and that is why books for them should be the first messengers of peace. They are to be collected into an exhibition which will tour Germany and then, perhaps, other countries as well. We are asking particularly for picture books, or at least heavily illustrated ones, to help overcome the language barrier. But we also hope to make available the literature that just tells a good story for the group work we plan to do. We hope German publishers will be able to obtain the translation rights for many of these books.

'Also, we would like to ask your country for drawings and paintings done by children. The pictures will speak an international language and will cheer children everywhere.'

At the close, a long military address!

This letter was sent to twenty countries in various languages and always in several copies. In spite of my optimism, I well knew that the International Exhibition of Children's Books project was, at most, still in the embryonic stage.

During the day I was assigned to the publications team, then concerned with the licensing of publishers. There was opportunity in plenty to make psychological observations, but I'll just mention one for what it is worth: most Americans plunged into their work with fanatical energy, they wanted to set German publishing back on its feet as quickly as possible. But Information Control was responsible for other matters as well, such as the re-establishment of a German radio service.

The story of how the first woman radio personality was discovered is not without charm, throwing light as it does on the way things were at the time.

Life at headquarters was lived behind barbed wire. The villa my room was in faced the entrance gate, and the view from my window looked directly out at the wire maze.

Unescorted women were not allowed to venture out in the evening. There were complicated regulations about permits and prohibitions, all of which boiled down to 'Don't get caught.' Still, it was quite impossible for a woman to slip past the barbed wire gate at night without a male companion. Two white helmeted MPs demanded to see passes, and when they were in a particularly sour mood because they were on night duty, every car was turned inside out in a hunt for female joyriders. Therefore, strictly speaking, the U.S. Army demanded that you, as a woman, find a boy friend for the evening if you didn't want to sit at home and scrub away like Cinderella.

Anyway, one night one of the big shots from headquarters took me along to visit a Homburg physician in his home, and he used a special pass to cover me.

We arrived at a beautiful, well-kept house that had not been taken over by the Army. The hostess, a doctor herself, took our wraps, her eyes twinkling behind her glasses. Later, after we had become good friends, she admitted to having guessed how uncomfortable I must have been in my uniform that night.

Our host was a gynaecologist, the director of a hospital, president of the medical society, and a resourceful and witty man. He at once began a lively conversation and from the cellar brought out a bottle of wine which he opened with a surgeon's skill. One subject after another was discussed candidly and at length. There were no false notes – sitting around that table we all immediately understood one another.

What interested me especially were the things said about women. There were a great many around, apparently, who still had not forgotten their dead Führer. The hostess had a dry sense of humour that cut through everything instantly, and her talent for describing people and situations was remarkable.

The thought then crossed my mind that this woman would make a crack director of a woman's radio programme. But she was a doctor, and people who chose this profession usually did so out of dedication. But why not try to get her for a limited time, I thought. When I asked her, after getting together a few more times, if she would be interested, she laughed hilariously. Write? No! She couldn't put two words together. And as for speaking – whatever made me think she could?

But I knew she had something to say, and a great facility for expressing herself.

'Should we make a stab at it?' I persisted. And she didn't say 'No.'

Since I couldn't invite her to headquarters, she had to sneak through the barbed wire after dark. Then we sat in my room, while I filled her in on the mysteries of broadcasting. She was quite an apt pupil.

Later, this time officially, we rode in a service car to Radio Frankfurt, now *Hessischer Rundfunk*. A friend from my London wartime days was there, Professor Golo Mann, with whom I'd already discussed the whole affair. Gabriele Strecker was given over to his care, with a four-week schedule of programming ahead of her. In a short time she became the radio star of the American zone, and a credit to her new profession.

It would be a sin of omission not to set down a few more glimpses of life at American headquarters. To a confirmed individualist like myself, it was a way of life which was peculiarly fascinating.

One morning I decided that the olive drab sameness of my uniform needed a fresh touch, so I exchanged the regulation khaki shirt for a white blouse. I managed to get past the mess sergeant, all right, but then in the dining hall sat down at breakfast opposite a colonel. Now I had to stick it out whether I wanted to or not.

Nothing at all happened at first. We spoke pleasantly, nobody batting an eye. Not even the colonel. At last, when we were finished, he turned to his adjutant. 'I guess I'd better go see the eye doctor,' he said. 'Something is wrong with my vision. I keep on seeing white instead of olive drab. To put it mildly, it's rather strange.' Then he winked and disappeared. No doubt he could hear our laughter following him. That was my inglorious attempt to reform the American Army uniform.

An anonymous benefactor, as a Christmas gift, gave me enough material for a made-to-measure officer's uniform. I had it done by a tailor who lived in a small cottage in Bad Homburg, and who had worked for the house of Hohenzollern. The uniform fitted like a glove and had so many personal touches that it was more like an elegant tailored suit than a uniform. I still have it today.

A less pleasant side of life at headquarters was the way we used to stuff our pockets full of cake and sweet things during meals, to hand out afterwards to starving children. The duty-sergeants had the strictest orders to permit no such thing, and their eagle eyes could find any unnatural bulge in the uniform. Everything found was confiscated on the spot – or almost everything. It's astonishing how inventive smugglers can be, and how rewarding were the happy eyes of children.

The story went around that for hygenic reasons all left-overs from the officer's mess had to be thrown away; half loaves of white bread, sausages and ham, canned goods hardly touched, fruit, vegetables, milk, even coffee. And this at a time when all these things were beyond the wildest dreams of the German people.

At the same time, of course, American food was being distributed regularly to the Germans, though its proper value wasn't always appreciated. Thus the belief went round that the only reason grapefruit juice – little known in Germany – was given away was because it 'tasted so absolutely obnoxious, and the Americans threw it out.' Similarly with sweet corn, a favourite dish served at American festive occasions. 'Corn is for feeding chickens,' said the wretched people who supposedly were being helped but actually felt persecuted. There was an endless string of such misunderstandings. Time alone has gradually cleared them away.

Just how much depends on such apparently insignificant incidents is impossible to measure, but it is hardly much different in politics. These are the petty things that cost most people their sleep.

I will always remember Christmas Eve, 1945, at U.S. headquarters. For the officers' mess there was a Christmas tree that towered to the ceiling, with electric candles, paper chains, funny hats from Lenten festivals, and mistletoe for the traditional kiss. There was stuffed turkey and sweet potatoes and cranberries and flaming Christmas puddings, for this was the first peacetime Christmas after long years of war. In spite of everything, most of those celebrating would rather have been at home sitting around their own tables.

The DPs (Displaced Persons) as usual waited on the tables. They hurried back and forth with dishes, but whenever you caught a glimpse of their eyes you could see how lost they were.

After dinner the circle broke up, but suddenly I spotted a piano in the corner. All the beautiful Christmas songs waited to be sung. I sat down and played 'Silent Night'. Then something happened that burned itself into my memory.

The DPs dropped whatever they were doing, crowded together round the piano, and began singing, all voicing the same song, but in a different language. Two harmonizing voices first, then three, until finally the Americans came over and sang along with them. Tears streamed down many faces, the strangeness was washed away. In its deepest sense, the miracle of Christmas was being reborn.

It's impossible to speak of that period without mentioning the PX, which played an important role at headquarters. Quite simply, the PX is the shopping centre for American military personnel who are stationed in a foreign country. At that time, U.S. civilians, members of the diplomatic corps and of international organizations, and exchange professors also were admitted into its sacred precincts.

Customers were waited upon by *Frauleins* who were surprisingly fluent in American English, slang included – thanks to GI boy friends more than to the courses set up to teach them the language. An American sergeant stood at the entrance, a Cerberus on guard against any of the new tricks constantly being dreamed up by unwelcome intruders.

For those who did gain entry, an incomparable quarter of an hour was in store. A big bag could be filled with delicacies: chocolate, sweets, condensed milk, coffee, tea, sugar, tinned goods, cigarettes, fabrics, underwear, and clothing of all kinds could be had. All imported direct from the States, their vibrant colours attesting to the optimism of the continent they came from. No one needed to be a detective to pick out those on the street who had been outfitted from the PX. This, no doubt, is how a large part of the German population came to be Americanized. And a quick check of the legs of the younger and gayer women around would have shown that nylon stockings were the order of the day. The coarse, ugly stockings of the *Bund Deutscher Mädel* at last were thrown away.

After pausing for a pick-me-up at the Snack Bar, people would drag their booty to the door. Now the second act began. There would be children waiting there mostly, but adults, too, and you could scarcely blame them. They were forbidden to collect there. We were forbidden to give them PX rations. But it happened, and right out in the open.

I noticed time and again how strictly the U.S. military stuck to the rules, and yet how they understood the crucial moment when it was necessary to close their eyes and give way to feelings of common humanity. There also, naturally, were bureaucrats who rigidly followed the letter of the law, and, also naturally, these precisely were the ones German opinion fastened upon, criticizing them and attributing their attitude to Americans in general.

Countering the PX was the black market, where many of the delicacies of the PX turned up at fantastic prices. A black market probably is unavoidable in times of crisis. This one disappeared with the currency reform, having run its course once everything could be bought openly in the stores.

It was common knowledge where and how the black market operated, but surprise raids could, at most, only check its progress. Indeed, there were times when the black market was a godsend in a country devastated by burning, bombing, and plundering. Is there really a German who never used such a channel for cigarettes, flour, coffee, tea, or, above all, for medicine? And is there really anybody among the occupying troops who never, in one way or another and often for the best of motives, gave in to the temptation?

But there was an even blacker market, not in a few cigarettes or a tin of Nescafé, but in truck loads of smuggled goods. The law had every reason to crack down on this with the severest measures possible.

Thinking back on that time, it must not be forgotten that all ideas of decency and morality had been turned topsy-turvy. Then, a German woman would walk along the streets and barter herself to get her family the barest necessities; a Balkan Jew whose whole family had been gassed could justify himself, saying, 'Anything I want to do here I can do.'

The only answer was in creating conditions that had some semblance of order as soon as possible. And one thing more – to save the children from danger surrounding them on all sides.

iii

Meanwhile, I waited at headquarters for the reaction to my letters. The postal situation was still in a primitive state, a letter from Bad Homburg to Zürich often taking as long as five weeks. The marvellous efficiency of the army postal system made America seem a great deal closer.

Finally one morning the first letter arrived, from France. I remember holding it in my hands a minute, unopened. The general's sceptical words rang in my ears, and all the audacity of this project rose before me.

The letter was what could be called a *document humain*. It came from the ministry in charge of such affairs, stating that France was prepared to co-operate and had sent letters out to its publishers. When enough books had come in, they would be examined by specialists and sent on.

I ran past all the outer office secretaries and directly into the general's office, carrying the letter before me like a flag. He shared my joy over the arrival of this first dove of peace.

The weeks and months ahead brought letters from everywhere, all assuring us of help. There was a pathetic answer from little Norway: many of her children's books had been casualties of the war, and even the publishers had no copies left. The fascinating idea was then hit upon of asking Norwegian children themselves to rummage through their bookshelves. Similar letters came from Holland – the land of Anne Frank – from Denmark, and Italy. England, land of children's books *par excellence*, hoped to give an especially fine collection; so did Switzerland, always standing in common cause with all nations. Of twenty countries contacted, nineteen promised their wholehearted support – it was overwhelming. Only one country refused. 'Twice we have been invaded by the Germans,' they wrote. 'We regret that we must refuse you.'

This letter arrived one night in February, at a time of year when springtime could be sensed in the air. How could I reconcile myself to such a decision? No nation could stand aloof when the earth itself was being renewed. I sat down and wrote another letter at once:

'I beg you to reconsider your decision. Yours is the very country that we need as we try to provide the children of Germany with a fresh start. Is it not in your interest even more than others to help educate a generation of Germans who may guarantee that a third invasion need never be feared?'

I was not disappointed. The Belgian book consignment was among the best of the exhibit.

There still was plenty of time before the books themselves would arrive, so I began looking around for buildings to house the exhibition in. The task looked hopeless. So many people were homeless in the bombed cities that it was futile even to try counting them. If an exhibition hall did exist, it would have been turned into a refugee camp. Any exhibition of children's books would be next in line, perhaps, but solid walls and electricity and heat all would be needed. What luxury these things were in Germany, 1946! The ghosts of the ruins even roamed through my dreams.

My crusade for international understanding through children's books began at that time. Mounting my hobby-horse, I charged into battle.

The first stop was Munich. Even at that time people sensed that this city was destined to become the intellectual centre of the Federal Republic, in spite of its bad reputation as the 'capital city of the Nazi movement'. Munich was the one place where the ruins of war took on the beauty of the ruins of antiquity, perhaps because of the blue windswept sky, or the clusters of trees which grew in the most surprising places under the blue sky. The reasons for this feeling were impossible to pin-point, but you were constantly being struck by it.

However, anybody who did search for the answer was impressed in a completely different way by the *Haus der Kunst*, called, in local dialect, 'Hitler's Bavarian Sausage Temple.' The American officers' mess was located in its pseudo Greek halls, and here was the official dining and meeting place for the American community.

You had to walk through a columned ante-room to reach the dining hall proper, which was always garlanded in a great show of decorations befitting the season – with garish paper wreaths and hollowed pumpkins, tinsel angels dangling from the ceiling, big candles with holders of *papier mâché*, or a Walt Disney jungle for the children. American gimmickry certainly could hold its head up amidst Hitler's brand of luxury.

Yet this *Haus der Kunst* had escaped destruction. I wondered if there weren't a deeper significance here. Pondering this, I was suddenly illuminated with the fact that it had been spared deliberately to house the first International Exhibition of Children's Books! At once I started looking at the exhibition rooms with a critical eye, and marched through all the halls as though they were already our property. In my mind's eye I swept aside all obstacles as mere debris. Children's books from all over the world would move into this temple of idols and their innocence would banish the evil spirits!

Carried away, I began writing a stream of memos, for by then I had learned that memos were the key to military and civilian administration. Most important, one must not lose patience.

In countless cases these memos had to be circulated on both sides of the Atlantic. And while the occupation authorities held the last word ultimately, usually they liked to consult the German authorities about such projects so that all concerned might work in harmony.

Vividly I could imagine how many military and unmilitary eyebrows were being raised, but I trusted in the magic of children's books. So the memos made their rounds. And I made mine – a method that has never failed me yet.

[45]

A most unusual event was the visit of Eleanor Roosevelt to the American zone early in the spring of 1940. She was an almost mythical figure whose humanity, intelligence and energy would have distinguished her even if she had belonged to an ordinary family. But she had been First Lady of America for so long, that, in a sense, she still was. I felt it imperative to awaken her interest in my project and count her among my allies.

All I needed was a lucky break, and I soon received one: an invitation to a press conference at the administration building of the military government in Frankfurt. Spick and span in my uniform, I ran up the stairs of the stodgy office building an hour ahead of time. The main hall was decorated with flowers stiffly arranged in official vases. My fingers itched to free them from their drill-like formation. The cream of the army government and the press already were assembled in the ante-room when a charge of excitement went through the air. Had the guest of honour arrived early? No, something unexpected had happened which demanded attention and a speedy decision to be made by somebody.

A German woman, who claimed that she was a schoolmate and friend of Eleanor Roosevelt's from her time in a Switzerland finishing school, wanted to speak to her classmate and offer her some flowers.

The journalists crowded round excitedly, their slightly raised noses sniffing a sensation. Perhaps this reunion would be just the thing to relieve the tension felt clearly by everybody. For the German press did not entirely share my regard for Mrs Roosevelt. Not only had she always been one of the bitterest opponents of the Nazi régime, but lately she had been speaking her mind on certain shortcomings of postwar Germany. The German reporters gazed at the schoolmate with looks that were positively affectionate. Meanwhile, the Central Intelligence division (the American secret service) was quickly investigating the schoolmate's past. They found nothing especially suspicious to work on. She had neither been a Hitler follower nor had she ever been involved in anything like an anarchist plot. She was asked to wait in an adjoining room until Mrs Roosevelt herself made the decision.

Mrs Roosevelt arrived on time and ascended the stairs with a galaxy of army people surrounding her. Light on her feet and with a regal bearing that her photos never reflected, her intelligent face was flooded with a radiant smile. A cosmopolitan woman, accustomed to being the centre of events, she nevertheless conveyed a naturalness that instantly drew people to her side.

A general could be heard telling her, in clipped phrases, the story of the school friend. 'Where is she?' Mrs Roosevelt said. 'Of course I want to speak to her.' And she broke through the official circle and hurried with open arms to her friend.

We stood aside and left the two to their memories. Suddenly they were girls again. exchanging secret thoughts in the finishing school at Lake Geneva. The changing expressions on their faces showed how much they had to say to each other. Several times Mrs Roosevelt touched her friend on the shoulder in a gesture of reassurance. Only when the general softly cleared his thoat, did this little scene come to an end.

The subsequent press conference threw up a lot of dust later, which wasn't a bit warranted. Kathleen McLaughlin, at that time foreign correspondent for the *New York Times*, introduced me to Eleanor Roosevelt. I sat across from her at the table and could hear every word she said.

Mrs Roosevelt had flown from London to Frankfurt, and it was the first time she had stepped on German soil since the end of the war. Her heart must have been filled with conflicting feelings. Germany had plunged the world into two wars, causing Mrs Roosevelt's country and herself personally great sacrifice. To look at President Roosevelt's photo at the Teheran conference was to see how the war had undermined his health. But, as ever, Mrs Roosevelt was willing to show understanding and relieve strain.

The American journalists deferred to their German colleagues – much depended on finding the right tone. Everything was going along smoothly until a German correspondent asked Mrs Roosevelt a completely ridiculous question.

'Don't you believe the children of Germany have suffered more than the children in the rest of Europe?' he said.

Eleanor Roosevelt replied through an interpreter, first apologizing for her poor German. Her eyes momentarily searched the reporter's face – she may have wondered if suffering ever could be measured, particularly that of children. Such a question must have seemed impertinent and painful to her, but she remained unruffled. In the soft, modulated voice she used throughout the conference, she said, 'How can I answer a question like that? I've just come from London and I've seen the children there. Their eyes, too, are full of suffering.'

That was it. She sat in silence as an argument broke out among the correspondents as to the value of such a question.

The next morning newspaper headlines, not only in German papers but in American ones, too, proclaimed something like this: MRS ROOSEVELT INSENSITIVE TO THE PLIGHT OF GERMAN CHILDREN.

Eleanor Roosevelt could hardly have been more surprised at such an interpretation put on her reply, for she discussed the incident with me right after the conference. The press people closed in on her, and I suddenly became aware that she was steering me gently by the hand to the other end of the room.

'Let's sit on this table,' she said. 'Maybe they will give us a little peace and quiet here.' And we hoisted ourselves on to the hard office table some orderly had shoved into the corner.

A memorable quarter of an hour followed. We tried to make sense out of the vicious, puzzling world about us. I did my best to give Mrs Roosevelt the whole picture of conditions in occupied Germany, quoting examples out of my own daily experiences. For her part, Mrs Roosevelt asked questions that showed how hard she herself was searching for the right answers.

I spoke to her about my idea of furthering international understanding through children's books. Her face lighted up with interest. I was disarmed to see how charming and vivacious that face really was.

'I like the idea,' she said. 'I like it very much. Please don't hesitate to tell me how I can help.'

Subsequently, never was I to ask Mrs Roosevelt for help or advice but that it was not given. Every letter was answered by return mail, and by her personally, not through the usual channels. Her name will be mentioned frequently in these pages.

This spring of 1946 in Germany! It seemed the quintessence of that season celebrated in so many forms by poets. Flowers poked their heads up in the fields of ruins. Never before or since have I seen such flowers. 'Weeds,' a companion said. I could have boxed his ears. Not even the children dared to pick the precious beauties, though their fingers trembled to hold them. But their fingers were not frozen any more, and the March wind played through their hair.

The most important cable arrived on March 29, 1946. PROJECT ON CHILDREN'S BOOK EXHIBITION APPROVED, it read. Along with it there came a query about the date of opening. It was a good thing I'd never had doubts about which way it would go, so that already I'd covered a lot of ground and could supply a date.

Generally, I am opposed to committees, but we would need one for this project. Ours was the first committee to team Germans with members of the occupying forces to get the job done. As we sat around the table suddenly we were no more than a circle of people, all intensely committed to bringing children together over a 'bridge of children's books.' There was a barrage of suggestions, many utterly utopian, but what difference did that make? One thing only mattered – we understood each other.

Before long, anybody passing a workroom in the *Haus der Kunst* would be surprised to see a bunch of enthusiastic committee members crouching over crates of books. Shipments had arrived from fourteen countries. Considering the particular moment in history and the state of the mails, nor to mention the constantly muddled communication lines people had to contend with, this was little short of miraculous. And once the exhibition began making its way across the war-torn world, even more contributions kept coming in.

While I was the moving force behind the exhibition on a part-time basis, my real job, which was still special adviser for women's and youth's affairs, demanded a great deal. Letters piled up on my desk in heaps every morning, and visitors waited in my room – children's book publishers who, though licensed, often didn't have the necessary training for their profession. They had to battle for every sheet of paper; printer's ink was as precious as gold. The paper they used for applications alone would have made a good number of book pages.

Editor's of women's magazines and producers of women's radio programmes were waiting too. Already there was a whole covey of publications such as *Sie* in Berlin, *Die Welt der Frau* in Stuttgart, *Frauenwelt* in Nürnberg, *Der Regenbogen* in Munich, and many others. These magazines needed material which the American Dana Service in Wiesbaden partly supplied. But never was it enough. Offices which had been set up for the German press in New York and London had to jump into the breach, as did the American Photo Service in Frankfurt.

How helpless many of these visitors seemed, and how uncertain in their behaviour. How unpredictable their reactions were! One day, out of the blue, a story would appear saying that the Americans were forcing propaganda material down the throats of the Germans. Actually, the opposite was true, for the Germans themselves were storming the Americans for material. Alas, much as one might wish, nations can hardly be put under analysis the way psychiatric patients are.

Part of a letter I wrote to a woman in charge of programming radio shows for women will throw some light on the problems that had to be faced.

'I think it is important to keep in touch with the questions that most occupy the German woman's mind at this moment. Only then can you help them with practical advice. I am thinking of things like the food shortage, the lack of housing and the housing taken over by the army, the problems of refugees and the problems of living in an occupied country. Above all, I am thinking of how to clarify for them what went on in Europe under Hitler.

'Denunciation is taking more and more alarming forms, with the battle between the German political parties aggravating conditions even more. Every effort must be made to speak of tolerance, a quality everybody expects of the occupying powers as a matter of course, but often failing to show it themselves.

'Most important, never forget the children. They are so very vulnerable to all these upheavals.'

On the margin of the carbon copy of this letter, I made a note: '*Epistola non erubescit*' (a letter does not blush). The last thing I wanted was a job as *Praeceptor Germaniae*.

But all the while that I was advising people, at Munich's *Haus der Kunst* hammers were pounding, American army hammers; paint was slapped on, from the French army; wet cleaning rags swiped over the floors, and bags of sugar were coming in from an English army contractor. The rooms were undergoing a thorough denazification. Not a trace of Hitler's time was to remain. One day I stood watching an academy professor passionately painting over the last evidence of a swastika, and the symbolism of his actions moved me. He guessed my thoughts.

'We should be chiselling it out, not painting it over,' he said, and we gave each other an understanding wink.

Then came the job of sorting through the children's paintings – a great day! They covered the parquet floor like mosaics. They were moving things, especially as documents, and you wanted to slip back into the *Haus der Kunst* under cover of night to secretly commune with them.

First there were the huge paintings done by children in

America, absolutely lush with colour – the best examples from the children's painting classes in the Museum of Modern Art in New York City. They came from a land that had been at war but had not been destroyed by it. The brushes of these little Americans had splashed over the paper in easy surges. The sky-scrapers were Walt Whitman poems turned into pictures. It was hard to tear oneself away.

On the other hand, the German children portrayed harrowing mirrors of gritty reality – the formats small, almost infinitesimal, every inch of space, each stroke of paint, something precious. Anxiety showed there instead of confidence; tiredness instead of energy. And what subjects! Ruins and more ruins, air raid shelters with tiny figures crammed together. There were scenes of refu-gees, broken bridges, somebody indulging in an orgy of wish-fantasy by showing an immense loaf of bread and slice after slice being cut from it, and there was a Cinderella in her fairy-tale gown at her wedding. And still in the memories of these children were the old market places, the fountains, and the town festivals.

Each zone of occupation was easily set apart by the work of these children; soldiers in their various uniforms, Yanks giving away chocolate; Tommies dressed in kilts; French colonials. From the Russian zone there were scenes of children on parade, in tent camps, standing in line for ration cards, and everywhere red flags fluttered in the wind. They were clean, clear, erased and redrawn, and you wondered if these pieces of paper had gone through a censor's hand.

The French children's pictures showed an inbred sense of colour, grace, elegance, and wit. Life in the country with geese, cows, the grape harvest, a castle with a personified bazooka peeping through a broken window. The feeling conveyed was of French youth shrugging its shoulders a bit superciliously, as though to say, 'C'est la guerre.'

Across the channel, the little English children covered their paper with giants in busbies standing outside Buckingham Palace, and larger-than-life portraits of Churchill. Others showed

[52]

small fishing boats on the beach at Dunkirk and, above everything, RAF planes hovering cloudlike in the sky.

The Pestalozzi Institute in Zürich, a centre for international children's paintings, sent the work of children living in a sheltered land. Cheerful and neat, many in pastels, not a line out of place. The world of their experience remained untouched, protected from the Furies of war. These pictures of mountains, villages, flowers, and animals, formed an oasis of blessed normality.

Strangely enough, Sweden, similarly a neutral country, showed a different aspect, but of course Sweden wasn't hemmed in by mountains, but rather lay wide open to the sea. To Swedish children, ships were always going out to sea with captains sporting grotesque beards, bright red noses, and shrewd eyes.

Children are blessed with an incorruptible eye, and unpacking these paintings was a continuing voyage of discovery.

July 3, 1946, marked the opening of the International Exhibition of Children's Books. Ten days earlier the military government had sent out fashionable invitations. My heart beat fast. Would the reality match my dreams?

But here I must quote from an article by Erich Kästner published in the *Neue Zeitung*, the American German-language paper, the day following. He leaped boldly over the official speeches and all the noted guests, for he had seen something more than met the eye.

'I wrote down the names of some of the distinguished people present and gladly pass them on to you. Among the gentlemen present were Herr Till Eulenspiegel, Baron Münchhausen, Tom Thumb, and the Pied Piper of Hamlin; Struwwelpeter from Frankfurt; Rübezahl the Riesengebirge; Monsieur Jean Bart from France; Lord Fauntleroy and messieurs Robin Hood, Robinson Crusoe, Gulliver, David Copperfield, and Oliver Twist from England; Kim from India, the Last of the Mohicans and Uncle Tom from the United States; a Steadfast Tin Soldier from Denmark, and several other well-known celebrities.

'Besides these gentlemen there were a good number of famous

animals: Puss in Boots, a little bull named Ferdinand, Mickey Mouse, Winnie-the-Pooh, Reynard the Fox, and Spiegel the Cat. Space does not permit me to give the full names and birth places of all the princes, kings, fairies, charcoal burners, pirates, witches, captains, heroes, and magicians who attended the opening, but maybe this summary recalls a lot of them to mind. Whosoever wishes to pay them a visit may do so. Their address is: *Haus der Kunst*, Munich, Germany. Open daily from 9 to 11 a.m., and from 2 to 5 p.m. Come as you are. Adults may tag along, too.'

Naturally, Emil and the Detectives were also among the guests of honour, and as their creator neglected to mention them, I shall. But let Kästner continue:

'. . . the International Exhibition of Children's Books not only affords a wide view of the differences and similarities in the children's literature of various nations, it also vividly shows the mutual influences they depend on. And there are historical curiosities to delight us, too . . .'

For one, part of a valuable collection of old European children's books was provided by Professor Rümann of Munich. Kitzinger's predominantly German collection brought the historical perspective up to more recent times, with its cut-off falling just before Hitler's seizure of power. Then there was a gap which Erich Kästner's critical eye immediately fixed upon:

'Something is missing – a selection of Nazi children's books which might have been set in a display case marked 'Adults Only.' In this way, the grown-ups present could have seen at a glance how far removed the Third Reich was from the path of common humanity.'

Should we really have given a place in this exhibition founded to further international understanding, to the hate books of Streicher and his contemporaries? Wouldn't there be more impact in such an exhibition formed by the Germans themselves? Perhaps Kästner was right and I was wrong. It is sad that no such exhibition has been held to this day, and sad not only for reasons of contemporary historical interest.

I cannot omit the end of Kästner's article, which contains an ironic illusion to the adminstrative problems the civic authorities had to contend with at the time:

'I was present when the foreign guests were being ceremoniously received. I sat in delightful company, right between Little Red Riding Hood and Sleeping Beauty. When the official functions were over, I escorted the two ladies through the rooms. Rübezahl was standing over by the window in lively conversation with the mayor of Munich. As we came up I heard the mountain spirit of Riesengebirge say, "You're certainly lucky to have us here, doctor!" "Lucky?" the good mayor asked, a little surprised. "Why, yes," Rübezahl said, smiling. "We don't eat anything, we don't drink anything, and we sleep between the covers of a book. We're just the kind of guests you like, aren't we?" At that he roared with laughter, and so did the mayor. But not quite so loudly. . .'

It was a beautiful, never-to-be-forgotten day, that July 3, 1946, especially in the afternoon when the doors opened wide to admit the children. In they streamed, in happy packs, their faces radiant as though they were entering the magic ring. Many came alone, others in the hands of adults. Their shoes were covered with dust, for they had come a long way.

Plenty of gloomy prophecies had been made, all expecting the worst from these children of the ruins. First, we had the books on loan only. The organizers of the exhibition had to assume a responsibility that nobody, in fact, could confidently assume. But this never gave me a moment's worry. Over the months that I'd been here, we'd become good friends, these children and I. Although a book at that time was worth its weight in gold, when the exhibition closed, more than a million visitors later, only a paltry small number of books had disappeared.

I could fill a book myself with the Munich exhibition. It was the first international event in postwar Germany, and so was of enormous political significance as well. Foreign travel still was financially and technically impossible for the majority of Germans, but here, by the means of children's books, they could visit many lands.

Long lines of people waited in front of the *Haus der Kunst* every morning, with all age groups and classes represented. The crowds were particularly large on Sundays when entire families arrived and strode over the polished floors. They warmed with laughter and excitement – you could never get your fill of them. The organizers were awarded so many spontaneous kisses by the children that they were almost smothered.

Once an old woman leading a child by the hand asked me, 'Aren't there any books of fairy tales without Hansel and Gretel in them?' I thought, 'What a strange question.' 'The child's parents died in Auschwitz, in the gas chambers,' she went on. 'Yes, in the witch's oven. And the connection between the two frightens me. This child was in the camp herself and escaped only by a miracle.'

I immediately realized that the ancient arguments about the cruelty in fairy tales now had to be weighed from an entirely different angle. This generation of children playing around me right in these rooms already had met witches and devils, monsters and villains, in other guises. No bread to eat, no bed to sleep in, mothers and fathers dead – all this was grim reality to them. Many of them had never known anything resembling security, which is a natural suit of armour that shields children against the cruelty of fairy tales. How little we had anticipated this, and how extreme the danger of never being able to right this wrong!

On one occasion I was walking through the rooms with a brash Bavarian boy. Safe on his farm in the mountains, the war had passed him by.

'What kind of books do you like most?' I asked him.

'War books,' he said. 'I like them best of all.'

[56]

Such a reply left me hardly able to speak.

'But don't you know how terrible war is?' I said finally. Taking him by the arm, I led him to the nearest window. 'Look out there,' I said. 'What do you see? Ruins, ruins! Even the trees are ruined. Now tell me, haven't you had enough?'

The boy – I guessed his age at about twelve or thirteen – looked at me undaunted.

'The bombs, I don't like those,' he said. 'But, yes, I do like war.'

A week later I had an entirely different experience. One afternoon a gentleman came up to me and asked in faultless English if he might join the conducted tour, and I invited him along. There was an unusually large crowd that day, and we were surrounded by people. However, I went through my familiar routine, opening display cases and holding up books of special interest for all to see. A wave of happiness passed through me as it always did among the children and their books, and the old gentleman seemed to share this feeling. His frequent questions indicated his interest and also his understanding of the subject.

Soon Professor Held, Munich's noted city librarian, appeared, making his way through the groups of people who were entering at an alarming rate. He whispered to me, 'In case you haven't realized it, the gentleman next to you is Crown Prince Ruprecht of Bavaria.' We both laughed at my naïveté, and so did the people around us.

Later I had a private conversation with the prince. Crown Prince Ruprecht was in his late seventies, and as the head of the Wittelsbach family (at one time the rulers of Bavaria) had been raised in a multi-lingual atmosphere. Bavaria at that time being one of the cultural centres of Europe, one of the evening rituals he remembered was his mother telling him fairy tales in his nursery in English.

'I can't tell you how dismayed our family was to have Munich designated the capital of the Nazi movement,' he said. And I could well believe him.

Two days later the American military government phoned me. The widow of General Patton (the famed American general who had been killed a few weeks earlier in an accident) wanted to stop over a few hours in Munich, and visit the exhibition. She arrived around lunch time, in deep mourning, looking pale and tired. But the exhibition cast its spell over even her. Gradually her tensed features relaxed, especially when she discovered several friends from her childhood in the American section.

All at once she picked up the American edition of *Struwwelpeter*. 'Struwwelpeter!' she cried. 'How I loved this book. I know it by heart.' And she began to recite 'The story of the boy who would not eat his soup,' and 'The dreadful story about Harriet and the Matches.' Her recitations were word perfect.

I removed a valuable first edition of *Struwwelpeter* in its original language from a case and showed it to Mrs Patton. She stared at it in both shock and fascination.

'You don't mean to say that *Struwwelpeter* is a German book,' she said.

I couldn't deny it, and could only assure her that Heinrich Hoffmann had been underground long before Adolph Hitler's career began. I also said that many of the best children's books had been translated into all languages and thus had become the common property of children throughout the world. The children had made them their own and had forgotten the lands they came from.

The twentieth century being the age of the questionnaire, we had to try it, too. Questions were framed around the general lines of, 'Do you believe in the idea of furthering international understanding through children's books?' 'Which six books do you like most?' 'Which books in a foreign language do you suggest be translated?'

Then the answers: 'What good is an exhibition at a time when no ordinary person can even buy a book?' 'At last, an effort to rescue us from our semi-barbaric state of illiteracy!' 'This

[58]

exhibition is an island of peace and happiness in the midst of a dying Europe. But do you really imagine anything can check its fall?'

Which books received the most votes cast by children and the young people themselves? Cooper's *Leatherstocking Tales*, Mark Twain's *Tom Sawyer* and *Huckleberry Finn*, Swift's *Gulliver's Travels*, Kästner's *Emil and the Detectives*, Selma Lagerlöf's *The Wonderful Adventures of Little Nils Holgersson*, Grimm's and Andersen's fairy tales, Johanna Spyri's *Heidi*, Schweizer's *Marie Luise*, Collodi's *Pinnochio*, Malet's *Homeless*, Harriet Beecher Stowe's *Uncle Tom's Cabin*. These represent only a portion of those voted upon, but they do show a surprisingly sound judgment. Naturally, children of picture-book age couldn't be expected to fill out the questionnaires, but the books themselves gave eloquent testimony to their popularity. Battered copies of Fischer's *Pitschi*, Elizabeth Beskow's *Hänschen im Blaubeerwald*, Carrigiet's *Schellenursli*, de Brunhoff's *Babar*, Hoffman's *Struwwelpeter* – all were fingered so lovingly by children's exploring hands and covered with such adoring kisses!

Even as the exhibition sailed to its climax in Munich, future exhibitions had to be prepared. In Munich we had been lucky to have found the *Haus der Kunst* intact. Now, though, a new task confronted children's books, that of creating the first cultural centres in the bombed cities.

I travelled to Stuttgart and Frankfurt, throwing out feelers. That's rather a metaphorical expression for a quite earthy assignment. I would like to have obtained the services of a 'Miss Children's Books' to charm the American military, the mayors, city planners, and library directors. I had to use different methods, but I had the advantage of knowing that behind me marched invisible throngs of children urging me on. Something had to move these bureaucrats. Surely they had hearts, no matter how crusty those hearts might seem.

In my brief-case I had all the data in black and white. Earlier, I had already staked out likely places. In Stuttgart the Württemberg State Library had caught my eye; in Frankfurt, the Städel Museum. Both were in ruins, and in both cities housing for the homeless and for refugees had to be found before anybody could think of rebuilding cultural institutions.

I assured the authorities that this international exhibition was, as an institution, exceptional. I painted a glowing picture of what a boon it could be to their cities. Not to mention, I added, that we would be leaving behind us a building restored and ready to use for future cultural events. They would have to have been made of stone not to agree, and they were not that certainly.

In Stuttgart the entire Swabian government aligned itself on our side. So did the American military governor, Col. William W. Dawson, whom the Swabians, royalist by nature, had practically installed as successor to their last king. He probably had no idea that he was occupying a throne, but he felt an awesome responsibility for the state he governed. When he died in office, far too young, all of Württemberg turned out to mourn him in public tribute.

The director of the Württemberg State Library, Dr William Hoffmann, was overjoyed on hearing the news that his library was going to be rebuilt to house our exhibition. The speech made by a teenager at the opening ceremony, August 20, 1946, was worthy of note:

'German youth today finds itself in the position of a traveller who, after completing a dangerous journey through a region of rocks and debris, has survived the night, perhaps, but he still cannot see what lies before him. We who have had to search through the narrowest boundaries of the spirit for our development, now depend entirely upon the free world to teach us all that has been withheld from us. Endless difficulties face us as we strive to grasp the international way of thinking, without forgetting that which is of worth in our own country. We have to wait for the world to take the first step, and that, I believe, is what it has done here, in this international exhibition, the first on German soil. How significant and encouraging it is that people from so many and so various nations have joined together to show us young Germans the true unity of all spiritual and moral ideas, as a reminder and a consolation. The young people of Germany, through me, thank you for this ray of light . . .'

One day a phone call came for me from the military governor of Hesse. He surprised me, as I was drawing up plans for the Frankfurt show.

'This is Colonel K . . . . speaking. Can you hear me?'

I could, of course, and at once recalled a still young, energetic colonel I had met once at a cocktail party. He was known for his thoroughgoing efficiency, which I was about to get a taste of for myself.

'Now I want you to listen,' the voice went on, disregarding the static on the line. 'Before you come to speak to me about the International Exhibition of Children's Books, I want to make one thing clear. Everything here goes 'through channels', by the book. Everything must be applied for in writing. Do you get that? In writing!'

'Certainly, colonel. I'll do the best I can,' I said.

The static crackled through the line again, and it occurred to me that the phone was on my side. So I was encouraged to add, 'I apologize, colonel, but I'm such an incorrigible individualist. . . .'

There now began a delightful, if strenuous, period of my career. I mounted my jeep once more, and the next day was standing on the bridge over the Main river looking across at the Städel Museum. I held no illusions – the Städel *was* a dreary sight. I then visited the colonel at his military government offices in my role as a female Machiavelli. First, I asked innocently enough to borrow a secretary 'to help prepare applications for the restoration of several rooms in the Städel Museum for the exhibition.' I used my best official jargon, and just hoped to master it in time.

The colonel looked at me uneasily, sensing my irony. Finally he said, 'Please put that in writing.'

[61]

'Fine,' I said. 'I'd be grateful, though, if your office would take care of that for me. I'll need a sample form to go by.'

Then I drove straight to Frankfurt's Mayor Kolb and his architect, Josseau, already busy with designs for restoring the *Goethehaus*. Soon we were busy on our underground plans.

People in the know, of course, perfectly well understood that the most carefully worked-out documentation would never produce the building materials in time. 'Army channels' – in other words, red tape – is by no means express service. The password was: 'Help yourself, then the army will help you.'

Probably the U.S. Army doesn't know to this day how high its credit stood among the German people then. I had only to say, 'We've got requisitions in with the U.S. Army, but we need wood, bricks, tiles, glass, window frames, cement, paint, nails, *now*. There's no better creditor than the American Army, and you will get your money in a few months' time.' They nodded in agreement. 'They' meaning architects, foremen, construction workers, tradesmen and, of course, the authorities. Improvisation was still greatly respected in postwar Germany. And this international project for children was a heady tonic for everybody who participated in it.

A point of honour was made of overtime. Who could think of an eight-hour day then? It was a magnificent late summer. The leaves of the trees were just beginning to turn, and their changing colours were mirrored in the waters of the Main. The poster figure of Little Nils Holgersson riding over the building site was clearly visible, and seemed to be waving to the people of Frankfurt.

Two days before the opening, the architect Josseau himself stole into the Taunus – at night, as befitted such a dark deed – to procure the panes of window glass we had ordered. There were still many army control points then, and window panes for a museum are not the easiest item to smuggle. However, it was managed, and once again I seemed to hear the rustling of our guardian angel's wings.

[62]

Everything gleamed with a festive air on opening day, Wednesday, October 1, 1946, a date of quite special significance. One newspaper wrote:

'In Nürnberg, sentences were pronounced after months of war crime trials. On the same day in Frankfurt, an International Exhibition of Children's Books was opened. . .'

The opening speech was made by my colonel, who showed that his bureaucratic instinct went no deeper than his uniform. He believed, he said, in the expression of life's natural powers and in the organic growth of the human spirit.

The exhibition itself was described by other speakers as 'the finest expression of the cultural and artistic evolution of the entire western world,' and 'a confession of faith in life that excludes fear and horror, not because it is ignorant of them, but because it refuses to believe in them. The future of the world will not be built by men who love danger because it is danger, but by those who overcome danger because they despise it.'

I stood in a corner, trembling with delight. Perhaps I ought to mention the conversation that took place between the colonel and me that day.

'You see, goals can be achieved by taking the official way, too,' he said.

'Oh, Colonel, not a single nail so far has come through your "channels," ' I said.

Berlin. As I write, not a day goes by without the name of this city being mentioned in connection with world politics. This divided city has become a seismograph recording the state of world peace. However, conditions then were a lot different, and crates of children's books were being prepared for their appearance there. Future problems were looming on the horizon, but then there was no iron curtain.

I remembered a cocktail party held in the Russian headquarters in Berlin. I sat at one end of a sofa, shy and ill at ease; the champagne was not all that was chilled. Speaking to a Russian cultural attaché through an interpreter, I risked asking why no Russian books had arrived for the exhibition. My Russian shrugged; he knew nothing. I cannot understand to this day why the Russians allowed this opportunity to go by, when they might have paraded the best of their children's books. They possessed a rich children's literature, and their gay and colourful fairy tales and picture books were a feast for the eye. Had they been sacrificed to party politics? Even the fabled Russian caviare left a sour taste in the mouth in the air that prevailed at that reception.

Berlin itself was starving and shivering with cold. Wet snow fell on the roof of the U.S. Information Centre which we'd selected to house our show. The economic distress was more critical in Berlin than in any other German city. The women of the ruins, who were dressed in the fantastic patchwork of their clothes, set the tone. Their hands toughened and swollen from the cold, their feet buried in German or U.S. Army boots, they laboured over the rubble. They were grey with hunger and deprivation, these 'women with the brooms,' and with their mouths set bitterly they lacked entirely any feminine grace. Famous as the Berliners were for their wit, they scarcely replied when you spoke to them. Hitler had robbed them of their sense of humour. And these were the mothers of the children who would visit the show.

The children themselves were miserably undernourished little creatures. They no longer played among the ruins but, scared off to other haunts, they hugged the walls and rubbed their cold fingers.

On the morning of December 6, 1946, opening day, a small girl unwittingly gave the shortest and best speech I ever heard. Seeing Santa Claus and his reindeers and sleigh decorating the wall, she stopped suddenly and caught her breath. 'Oh, now it is peace,' she said. And again, 'Yes, now it is peace.'

The Berliners took the exhibition to their hearts immediately. Were former Nazis admitted? This question came up continually. Ought we to act like Nazis in reverse, admitting only those who had *no* party card? This would have completely corrupted the spirit of understanding we wished to foster. So anyone, anyone who wanted to come, would find the door open.

In any event, we'd learned long before not to probe too deeply into the past of our well-wishers.

Das Börsenblatt für den Deutschen Buchhandel, the trade magazine of the German book industry, had not yet been moved from its traditional home in Leipzig. It devoted a remarkable edition to the Exhibition which today is a collector's item. Agreeing wholeheartedly that 'books have the superior function as a means of intellectual exchange,' the editors at the same time regretted to have to record that the USSR was not represented.

They wrote: 'The absence of the many instructive and, for the most part, quite realistically mannered Soviet books, including such masterpieces as Tolstoy's "Three Bears," can only be deplored, especially when one considers the facilities the Exhibition offers for comparison.'

We shared these sentiments entirely, and also the writer's conclusion that 'this exhibition of children's books, in spite of the absence of the Soviet Union and other countries, demonstrates the bond that unites children of all countries, regardless of nationalistic boundaries.'

There was no questioning the fact that the Exhibition acted as a substitute for the Christmas fair, and it became harder than ever to turn down children who begged for books. I was sitting on the steps all alone one night with Munro Leaf's *Ferdinand the Bull* on my lap, wondering how I might acquire some books for the children's Christmas presents. Ferdinand gave me an idea.

Every day newspapers were published in Berlin, so there must be a huge stockpile of newsprint some place. If somebody would only print *Ferdinand* on newsprint, and by folding make it into a book, the children's Christmas wish could come true.

I immediately thought of the Berlin librarian, Dr Moser, now director of the American Memorial Library in Berlin. He'd thrown himself headlong into our plans for the Exhibition and was just the man! That same day we began putting in urgent applications for permits to the military government, and that night, while snowflakes fluttered through the air, *Ferdinand the Bull* became *Ferdinand der Stier*. Munro Leaf had written so beautifully about the bull who didn't want to fight that it was not an easy job to render the story into another language. Often, when I was at a loss for the right word, I would gaze at the picture of Ferdinand as Robert Lawson had drawn him, and in no time my pencil would be flying over the page.

The printing presses at Tempelhof spat out 30,000 copies in one night. A few days before Christmas I stood at the entrance to the main exhibition hall with *Ferdinand* under my arm, feeling as carefree as Ferdinand himself. The children reached eagerly for their copies of the book. They loved the funny illustrations and already were deep in reading as they walked away.

Ferdinand was a spectacular success. His creator should have won the Nobel Peace prize. Soon the story of Ferdinand could be heard being told on every street corner in Berlin. The first edition was out of print in the wink of an eye, and not even a copy remained for the files. We paid dearly to buy some back from the black market, where *Ferdinand* finally wound up as a prize object.

'And what did you do about the copyright?' a publisher asked me some time later. The copyright? Easy – we had simply forgotten about it.

There was another gift for the children. *Heute*, the American newspaper in Germany whose staff I'd recently joined as managing editor, at my urging published Clement Clarke Moore's ' 'Twas the Night Before Christmas' in a colour reproduction, as a Christmas present. Erich Kästner was happy to translate the verses, and Emery Gondor did the illustrations. The issue was dedicated to the children of Germany with these words:

'This famous, adored American Christmas poem is more than 120 years old. The New York biblical scholar and children's friend, Clement Clarke Moore, wrote it on Christmas Eve in 1822 as a Christmas present for his own children. Through them, he gave it to all the children in the world. Even today, a procession of children gather on Christmas Eve each year to walk through the streets of New York with lighted candles, bound for the grave of Clement Clarke Moore, who with this poem made St Nicholas the friend of every child alive.'

Soon young and old alike, to a tune made up by themselves, were singing this classic:

> '*Now Dasher, now Dancer, now Prancer and Vixen!*
> *On Comet, on Cupid, on Donner and Blitzen!*'

I could see the team of reindeer dashing over the ruins of Berlin.

In fairy tales good things always happen in threes, and so one more surprise awaited the children. This was the showing of Walt Disney's film, *Snow White and the Seven Dwarfs*.

A favourite film of children in many lands, most German children knew of it only by rumour. The picture book version we had of it in the exhibition was so popular it was dog-eared. Occasionally you could hear the *Dance of the Dwarfs* being played on a scratchy gramophone.

But Snow White lay in her enchanted sleep in the safe of a Berlin bank instead of in a glass coffin. Negotiations between American and German film companies were at an impasse, and no Prince Charming had rushed to Snow White's rescue. Should I try?

I wrote to the legendary Mr Disney and received a prompt reply. Snow White was set free for Christmas film showings to the children of Germany, who welcomed her with squeals of delight. Then once more she was put back to rest in her glass coffin.

iv

Shortly after Christmas I got my travel orders to go full steam ahead to Munich and the job of editing *Heute*. 'Steam' literally, for on my way there by train a trail of black smoke streamed into my compartment from the resurrected engine. The military coach was jammed and in other carriages people were standing on the iron boarding steps. The train stopped even at the smallest stations to catch its breath. An amusing trip, but filled with question marks.

In Munich I was assigned to a villa, near Biederstein park, which had been taken over as quarters for the American personnel working on *Die Neue Zeitung* and *Heute*. I am sure occupation authorities cannot avoid seizing civilian housing, but such places certainly are hard to get used to. I kept imagining the spirits of the former occupants roaming through the rooms. It was quite clear that they could not be friendly spirits.

Every home taken forcibly this way meant a dozen enemies. In Munich alone a quarter of a million people had lost their houses and apartments and were camping in attics, wartime bunkers, and cellars. The remaining dwellings were immediately considered fair game for conversion into barracks. And you don't have to be a snob to object to army taste in furnishings – brown blankets and clumsy ash trays! Being a woman especially makes one recoil. For, after all, the army still is predominantly an institution of men.

The Biederstein house still held great charm, though, even if this function may have been far from the purposes its owner, a Bavarian nobleman, had envisioned for it. Luckily, I was installed in an isolated corner near the entrance hall, a square little room with a kind of glass veranda. No luxury apartment, perhaps, but it included running water – cold, of course. Since I would rather have cold water for my own personal use than be required to share hot water in the community bathroom, I was satisfied. Then I set to work as an interior decorator, putting children's paintings on the walls and getting a bookcase from the supply depot. A few borrowed pieces of antique furniture, known as the 'Biedermeier style,' conveyed a delightful sense of at-homeness. And I mean that, for it would be hard to count how many famous and ordinary people sat there in the green upholstered easy chairs and comfortably stretched their legs out under the tea table.

An adjoining general reception room was as good as unused, though it contained a beautiful grand piano. It could not provide much benefit to anyone because the occupants of the house each led such independent lives, and part of that independence, of course, was – for the American journalists – the inevitable girl friends.

Most of these girls were German and looked on the house as their particular domain. Here, making their *Amis* a cosy home, they themselves could come into their own. They decorated the rooms with cushions and flowers, darned socks (which seldom needed darning) and showed off their culinary talents in the kitchen.

Officially, the hosts of these girls were permitted to eat only at an American officers' mess or at the press club. But as good as those meals were, home-made food soon was keenly missed. So it became the practice to build up a larder from the commissary – the American army's supermarket. Then the girl friends could perform their culinary magic for them at home.

I was the only single woman legitimately staying in the Biederstein house and often I wanted to stay home and make myself an omelet. But when the girls immediately made it clear to me that they considered the kitchen was strictly theirs, I backed off. So many times this 'intruder' would fry an omelet at the most unusual hours. That is the way one learns to come to terms with a cockeyed world.

Among these women secretly lodging with us there were many sharply contrasting personalities. Most could not be considered 'loose'. Frequently they were recruited from among German office workers on the American military payroll, and most spoke at least a basic sort of English. There were war widows, daughters keeping a family above water, refugees from all ends of the earth. And among them, naturally, were others who were willing to risk any adventure for a pair of nylons or some American cigarettes. Exceptional circumstances demanded an exceptional adjustment of ideas, and I had no intention of meddling in these ticklish affairs.

The situation was most embarrassing when army authorities held a house inspection. Thanks to a top-notch grapevine network, word usually was spread around in time. This was where my lawful presence in the Biederstein house came in useful. Again and again a colleague would knock on my door with a load of women's garments in his arms and, smiling in embarrassment, ask if I would hide the things in my wardrobe. Finally there were so many clothes that my wardrobe – already a far too small and ramshackle piece of furniture – could have used rubber walls. Then if the inspector came he could calmly look through the newsmen's wardrobe and no tell-tale skirt would peek out among the olive drab.

A story went round about an especially perceptive inspecting sergeant who, in a similar case, found four pairs of women's shoes so different in size that, once discovered, they naturally would draw questions. He lined them up on the floor. The woman who managed the place said that, as he was leaving, he merely smiled and told her not to move them. What a sophisticated way to show without turning in a report that he knew what was going on!

Heute was billeted, together with *Die Neue Zeitung*, in the former *Völkische Beobachter* building in the Schellingstrause in Munich. It was an ugly structure, patched up for its new purpose but only, as it were, for a gesture. Buildings, like people, have characters. It seemed grisly to know that the paper for American publications now was running over the same drums as those used by the *Beobachter*. Had the sound of goosesteps really died away? Or, if one listened hard, could they not still be heard on the stairways and in the corridors?

The managing editor of *Heute* at that time, Heinz Norden, a smart and capable man, headed an extraordinary team. Every German photographer of rank was at his disposal: Bernd Lohse, Herbert List, Hilmar Pabel, Hannes Betzler and many more, as well as assistance from *Life* and *Look*, and *Harper's* and *Vogue*.

And journalists of the first rank were on the editorial staff of *Die Neue Zeitung*, one floor below: Hildegard Brücher, Walter von Cube, Luiselotte Enderle, Martha Maria Gehrke, Egon Jameson, Erich Kästner, Walter Kiaulehn, Robert Lembke, Bruno E. Werner, and from the other side of the Atlantic was work from Thornton Wilder, James Thurber, Carl Sandburg, and Walter Lippmann.

Heute and *Die Neue Zeitung* had the mission of instructing their German readers on daily events and also presenting the United States as the land of democracy. Of course, anyone could find the cloven foot in this assignment. But since the all-powerful 'chief' was ensconced on another continent, an amazing amount of freedom was exercised by the editors. And rightly, for they were the ones living on German soil, gathering their stories first-hand. Sometimes bristling cables flew across the ocean, but the system managed to survive.

No gala *première*, no matter how dazzling, could compare with the editorial conferences on either publication, and at every session it was in a *première* mood that I sat down in my chair. Lightning wits flashed back and forth until one was blinded. The masterly conductor of *Die Neue Zeitung*, Hans Wallenburg, was a veritable Von Karajan of journalism, a successor to the genius Hans Habe, who had created the paper at the end of the war.

Dressed in a major's uniform, Wallenberg was small and round

[71]

and burned with zeal to publish the best paper of the past, present, or future. Berlin and the Ullstein publishing house had moulded him and he was committed to their tradition. Although the Third Reich had taken away his home, position, relatives, and friends, he kept an objective view. He often took his German readers severely to task, but he never insulted them. He clearly realized that a past not coped with was bound to become an oppressive cross for them.

Many times the clock struck midnight while we were still in the office. Heinz Norden would have coffee brought up and served and no one thought of an eight-hour day. Meaningful work, then, was a blessing. Recent events were etched so vividly on the minds of our German associates that they sat behind their American army desks in their dyed uniforms and never looked at the clock.

Fantastic photographs crossed over my desk in those years. Extermination camps, gas chambers, faces of people who had been tortured to death. The pictures were all found by accident and sent in to the photo editor. But should they be made public? Had the time come to show the Germans what they had done, or was it past? This was not photo selection as an ordinary editor understood it; new circumstances ruled every choice. 'Should we run the picture down the side of the page from the top corner, Mr Winkel?' 'Should we put the picture at the bottom, Mr Winkel?' And Winkel, a German, a fanatic anti-Nazi and a highly competent newspaper man, moved the picture up and down, his hands trembling.

On the other hand, pictures from other countries couldn't be shown enough. Germany had walled itself in for more than a decade and had seen only what the authorities had allowed it to see: cities overrun with armies that immediately altered the faces of those cities; Notre-Dame no longer Notre-Dame so long as Paris lay under the Swastika banner, its windows without luminosity. Many have said so, those, naturally, who were opposed to the occupation. It was easily explained; their own inner eye had changed, not the windows.

Once, at Christmastime, *Heute* carried a children's painting, in colour, on the cover. It wasn't done without a fight. An indignant American colleague cried, 'A children's painting on the cover of *Heute*? Over my dead body.' And he waved a picture of a Christmas cover girl at us. Of course the children won. The painting showed a snow-covered village in the midst of a Christmas fair, and the words:

Stop telling us of war and destruction,
The children cry out
Across the boundaries
That adults establish.
And they press gloriously on
Into the uncharted future,
Creating again what the other
So mercilessly ruined.

The cover received special praise in a cable from Washington. *Heute* thus was a highly arresting attempt to define the real function of the tabloid press in our time. When it was discontinued by the military government, one wished to see it taken over by capable Germans. Not one of the countless tabloids that later shot up was able to fill the gap.

One night when I found it hard to fall asleep, I came upon the idea of collecting bedtime stories for children. There must be a hoard of such stories around, I thought, that would delight children and also afford adults glimpses into the world of the imagination. Excited, I sat down at my desk and composed an appeal I hoped *Die Neue Zeitung* would publish:

Goodnight Stories for My Child

' "... and now just one more story," children beg as they go to bed. A story is so needed at the close of a child's day.

[73]

'Even prosaic people become poets when they are sitting at a child's bedside. There are bedtime stories short and long, happy and sad. They tell the tale of the worm who lived in his apple house, and of the dish of vegetables the child would not want to eat — and there are countless variations.

'Material possessions may have been burned or destroyed by the war, but bedtime stories have survived the horrors and are waiting to be retold.

'Like the Brothers Grimm, *Die Neue Zeitung* wants to draw the stories out and put them in a collection. They are to be original writings, not derived from the published body of children's literature. They may be written in pencil on any paper at hand.

The best submitted will be published in *Die Neue Zeitung* and later anthologized in a children's book.'

Now I would have to warn my secretary, who would receive the first shock of the expected deluge. This might be the right place to introduce her. Mrs Ledig was born and raised in Saxony and excelled in all the virtues these people are noted for, not to mention that I had infected her early with enthusiasm for the idea of 'International Understanding Through Children's Books.' Her contributions towards building up the International Youth Library cannot be overlooked. Not even a hurricane could rattle her. Since I, in 15 years of working with her, was often myself that hurricane, I ought to know.

About 20,000 bedtime stories rained down upon us, exceeding our highest expectations. But with 20,000 such stories, how could we separate the good from the bad? Ten persons versed in bedtime stories got down to work that stretched over months, and it was rough going.

Bedtime stories are supposed to lull one to sleep, but our ten readers lost sleep. The stories ran rampant through Little Snow Flake, Little Elf, Little Hedge Rose, Little Dew Drop, Little Moon Beam. German sentimentality, which had survived the Third Reich and the Second World War, even sprouted new shoots!

The dangerous instinct of mankind, and of Germans particularly, to seek refuge from a monstrous reality by withdrawing into the unreal became apparent in these 20,000 bedtime stories. What was not apparent — and this was corroborated by psychologists who drew much significance from this unique material — was the new interpretation of events during the Nazi period. Not a single story made the slightest allusion to them!

Among correspondence accompanying the stories was a letter from a descendant of the Grimm brothers who expressed her thanks for 'the continuation of her forbears' life work'. I replied to her that the work of the brothers Grimm had never seemed more admirable to me than now.

A portion of the stories appeared in *Die Neue Zeitung*, then they were put into book form and translated into many languages. They were so popular that in January, 1947, Erich Kästner alluded to them on the stage in the Munich cabaret he had founded, '*Die Schaubude*' (The Display Booth). Two life-size, cardboard figures of children were set up onstage to listen to rather gruesome bedtime stories of a political commentator. The children just stared at him, blond, blue-eyed, and idiotic. Trying to cheer them, the commentator then offered, 'And now as a reward, one more story – a get-up-time story . . .'

The Animals' Conference also originated in the Biederstein house. I couldn't get the theme out of my mind. At the time, the number of international conferences that were failing grew with every month; it became an effort to remember them all. There was no telling, fortunately, how many others, equally abortive, still lay ahead of us.

Why were human beings still not capable of carrying on their affairs of state intelligently? I wondered. Here this beautiful planet called earth belonged to them, and what did they do? War! Again and again children were in danger of being killed in wars. Maybe it would be better to let the animals of the world have a stab at governing, matching their instinct against human reason. When I reached this point, I went to Kästner.

[75]

'Do you mean it would be a book for adults, or what is called a book for adults?' he said.

'Yes and no. I think it would have to address itself beyond children, to adults.'

'No easy venture,' he said. 'Children sometimes like adult books, but seldom the other way around.'

'But why not in a case like this? The theme touches everyone.'

'Yes, that's true,' he said.

Shortly afterwards a slim man dressed with casual elegance could be seen each evening wandering across Schwabing to Biederstein street – it would be Kästner – with a cat on his shoulder. Usually walking next to him was Lottchen, his wife, always ready to see the comical side of things. In the Biederstein house a bright, warm room had been converted to vintage Biedermeier, and was awaiting them.

'And Mickey came along, too,' I said of their cat, who hissed at me as I stroked him along the back.

'He's got the leading role,' Kästner replied in his faintly Saxon accent. 'How can we write about a conference run by animals without any animals?'

Mickey was set down gently on the white porcelain stove that hadn't been used since central heating, but he liked it there and immediately began to purr. If we got boxed into a corner on our work, Kästner would get up from his chair and walk over to the stove.

'Mickey,' he would say, 'maybe you know how to make some headway. Help us out of this mess.' And of course Mickey would do just that. He was not a member of a literary household for nothing.

When I think of those evenings my heart warms with affection. Outdoors it was winter, snowy and cold, but the first hints of a change for the better were in the air. We sat in our 'secure' security, drank wine, nibbled PX sweets, and tossed ideas at one another like balls. Our heads, it seemed, fairly blazed and crackled.

We decided that only Walter Trier could illustrate our book, because the theme touched him as closely as it did us. He was living then in Canada, so we wrote him and obtained his approval by return mail.

The publisher? Opi, naturally, whose name actually was Dr Emil Oprecht, the founder of Europa Verlag in Zürich. Writers in exile who suddenly found themselves in trouble always had got refuge, understanding, and encouragement from him.

Opi and his wife Emmie were legends, not only as bold publishers, but as philanthropists as well. How many refugees they had cleared the way to freedom for, how many children had eaten at their table and found a home with them during and after the war, was their closely guarded secret. *The Animals' Conference* would be in good hands with them.

Fortunately, we did have a rough draft in our hands. Now Erich Kästner began to write the book. With a blend of gravity and humour and an insight of the animal in the human and the human in the animal, he gave *The Animals' Conference* the humorous and touching tone that Walter Trier's illustrations imparted a special magic to. The book appeared in many languages, even Hebrew and Japanese. Perhaps men will yet take his Happy Ending to heart:

'When the people heard over the radio that their statesmen had given in to the animals and had signed the treaty for never-ending peace, such rejoicing broke out in the world that the earth's axis was bent half an inch. And when parents learned that the children were coming back as soon as all frontier barriers had been taken down, they raced to the boundaries and sawed the barriers to pieces. In their places they built arches of flowers and hung them with garlands. Even the officials helped eagerly. And now there was no more "this side" and "that side", and all shook hands with each other.'

Among the events planted especially deep in my memory of that early postwar period in Germany, was a meeting with students in the home of James Clark, then acting military governor of Bavaria. He and his warmly impulsive wife Ruth had broken out of the ghetto spirit that prevailed over many of the American occupation authorities and entered into more personal contact with the German people.

One evening in their home they gathered together about 25 students. All were decked out in their 'best', jackets either too big or too small, with wonderfully applied leather patches on the elbows. Darkly serious, defensive, they drank in silence the strong coffee served by the Clarks. Jim Clark himself cautiously opened a general discussion on the postwar life of German students, their problems and hopes for the future. Soon each speaker became inflamed with his own words: one after the other threw into the discussion 'The Beaten Fatherland,' 'The Occupation,' 'Housing shortages,' 'The cultural vacuum,' 'The destruction of all values.' There were few signs of anyone recognizing the real lay of things, but so much self-pity it almost made one gasp.

These scarcely grown-up people were still reeling under the shock of events whose origins and deep significance they did not in the least comprehend. But wasn't it up to the university, as one of its first duties, to try to come to grips with this situation? The most we could do was advise the young Germans to pull themselves out of their postwar misery by their own pigtails, as the free-spirited Baron Münchhausen had done – to realize that the building of Germany was a remarkable opportunity for them. Their generation had not been condemned, as had earlier ones, to making a way for themselves in a world brought to a standstill in every last detail. They had a wonderful chance to help reshape their own world.

Once these young people changed their attitudes, even the American occupation, which they didn't understand, had its positive side. Representatives of a great and powerful nation were living among them, willing to establish contact with them, and to exchange experiences. So wasn't it foolish to refuse this chance?

[78]

In a plain conversational tone we let them know our views.

Almost magically the expressions of our young listeners went through a change as the weight of their dejection, so visibly pressing on them before, suddenly dissolved. A lanky bespectacled student jumped to his feet and, at ease again, good-naturedly thanked us. We parted in cheerful spirits.

The next day a delegation of students showed up with a colourful bouquet of flowers. They had cycled out to the country (flower shops, of course, were deserted, for the currency reform had yet to come) to gather wild mallow and wood anemones and butterfly-like sweet peas.

Yehudi Menuhin's concert in Salzburg – here, for a moment, I must go back in time.

In London during the last years of the war, I belonged to the ABSIE – The American Broadcasting Station in Europe. It was a little brother to the powerful BBC. One day Menuhin appeared for a recording session of Mendelssohn's *Violin Concerto in E Major*, and I hid myself in a corner of the studio to hear him. The music awakened so many thoughts in me! Mendelssohn, as a member of the race persecuted and ostracized by Hitler, had been banned from the start. (Not only the living but the dead, too, were objects of Hitler's hatred.) I knew there were countless other people in Nazi Germany who yearned for this music.

After the concert I approached Menuhin and asked if he, providing the station management agreed, would consider playing for his fans in Germany, as I believed that many such fans existed.

Menuhin said without hesitation, 'Yes.' He asked me to write down a few introductory words for him to say in German. I still have the paper they were written on:

'I am playing Mendelssohn's *Violin Concerto* for all of you whose ears are still open to hear it. May Mendelssohn's music reach you ringing of solace and hope.'

Years later people in Germany were to tell me how they had

[79]

listened to the broadcast, at the risk of their lives, and how much it had meant to them . . .

Now, though, on August 13, 1947, Menuhin was standing on the podium of the old Festival building in Salzburg. He was playing not Mendelssohn but Brahms. Wilhelm Furtwängler was conducting the orchestra, not the brilliant and daring Furtwängler of the twenties, but an ascetic one, old before his time.

At Furtwängler's first appearance, conducting Hindemith's *Symphonic Metamorphoses*, an icy silence greeted him, for, rightly or wrongly, his audience felt that, politically, he had straddled the fence during the Nazi period. Then Menuhin grabbed Furtwängler's hand when he appeared on the stage to play – an unmistakable gesture! As their overpowering rendition of Brahms came to a close, the audience now responded with an ovation that was clearly for Furtwängler, too.

In the summer of 1946 I was invited to the 'Berchtesgaden Hof' in Berchtesgaden, by the general of the Information Control Division. A nice enough gesture, but the idea of visiting *der Führer's* favourite retreat made me shudder. It is not advisable to turn down invitations from generals, however, so I accepted with thanks.

My room had a magnificent view of the mountains. The maid appeared even without my ringing for her and offered her services. Delighted that I spoke German, she said passionately, 'Oh, madam, nobody around here speaks anything but English.' (Why should they not? This hotel was for the highest-ranking officers in the American Army). 'It was altogether different before,' the maid went on. '*Der Führer* used to stay here, Göring, Goebbels... Oh, those were the days. How gentle they all were (gentle!), and now we're treated like dirt. As if we had leprosy . . .'

I listened in growing amazement. Clearly, the moment for re-education had arrived. I gave this confirmed believer a lecture on contemporary history, expecting to open her eyes. Without any success at all.

'Oh, you didn't know those gentlemen, madam,' she said. 'People have given you a false picture of them . . .'

It was no use wasting any more time on such a person, even though officially that was part of my job.

An excerpt from a widely discussed article about General Lucius D. Clay, which appeared in the *Bavarian Review* in the autumn of 1948.

'In an occupied country the person of the military governor stands above good and evil. But he, too, is human, with all the weaknesses, failings, and worthwhile qualities natural to humanity. So, when those who represent the people of the occupied zone praise the governor and thank him without pointing out his failures, are they not necessarily open to suspicion of flattery, or even actual collaboration?'

For children, it was easier. Their thoughts were less complicated. One of their rope-jumping dialect verses went, '*Ein, zwo, dree, da kommt der Schenerel Klee.*' General Clay's air lift was the central point of their games.

CARE parcels worked magic in the post-war period. *Die Neue Zeitung* wrote:

'Suddenly the doorbell rings. The mailman delivers a card. The recipient is asked to report to the nearest distribution office for foreign parcels. A CARE parcel is there, sent to him from America by a friend or an unknown well-wisher. If his identity papers are in order, he can take the parcel along. With the family standing round to watch, the weather-proof wrapping is removed. It might be a parcel of food, or else blankets, or material for making dresses, suits, or children's clothing, together with the help of enclosed needles, thread and scissors.'

A stroke of genius, those CARE parcels. Many alleviated real need, others got to the wrong addresses or were turned into booty by the black market. On the occasion of her stay in Germany, Mrs Eleanor Roosevelt asked me:

'Is it true that the people receiving CARE parcels don't always turn out to be good neighbours? That on one floor the CARE parcels lie well-hidden under beds while on a floor below children are starving?'

Investigations proved that often this information was all too true. 'When will the German people learn to be good neighbours?' Mrs Roosevelt asked with a sigh – a concern many of the best Germans shared.

Later there were CARE parcels containing children's books. I was present in Washington when the idea was being considered. But how I happened to be in Washington is another story entirely . . .

I was sitting in my *Heute* office one morning and wondering how I could turn the International Children's Books Exhibition into an International Youth Library. This thought had occupied me constantly and I kept bringing it up in discussions. Moreover, I had a drawer full of letters pleading for such a library.

It would be ungrateful to insist that the generals, both the active ones and the passive ones, would not listen to this plan, for they did have other problems to consider. Often they looked at me in alarm, for it is not easy to diplomatically dodge a woman with a 'one-track mind.'

Anyway, one morning I was told that two Americans wanted to see me. In stepped two lanky men – this is the only way to characterize them – and introduced themselves as emissaries from the humanities section of the Rockefeller Foundation in New York City. They were on a fact-finding trip through post-war Europe to study conditions for themselves and draw their own conclusions.

How I would have liked to put my two visitors in a glass case and exhibit them around Germany: This is the way American humanists look! For in their minds the German had quite another picture of the *amis*. *Ami*, to be sure, was a charming expression, but often it was accompanied by a slighting tone which seemed to say, 'We Germans are, in spite of everything, far superior to you uncouth foreigners.'

These Germans would have been astounded to hear how shrewdly they were being summed up, how well these two Americans understood them. These Americans had few illusions – I almost began to be ashamed of my own – but they were determined to support Germany's efforts to build itself up again.

Then suddenly one of them said, 'We've seen the International Children's Books Exhibition in Berlin. We liked it a lot. It's one of the best things we've seen on our trip. The idea of international understanding through books for children and young people interests us. Tell us more about it.'

I had to swallow three times before I could begin. But then there was nothing for me to do but open my heart and mind to them; the only hard part was to hold back a flood. It was a wonderful fifteen minutes, but naturally, even as children do, I dipped the brush I painted the picture with deeper into the pink colours than the grey.

'Maybe we'll be able to help you somewhat,' the two men said in an understatement designed to bring me back down to earth. But all I could hear was a 'yes.'

'Send us a detailed plan for this International Youth Library with all the data on it you can get. You'll be hearing from us again.'

I was still beaming long after the two men had gone.

In spite of gloomy forebodings of boring my readers, one document I cannot suppress is the following memorandum:

31 May, 1947

TO: Colonel T., Director, Information Control Division, Military Government for Germany (U.S.), APO 742, U.S. Army.

PER: Colonel K., Chief, Information Control Division, Office of Military Government for Bavaria, APO 407, U.S. Army.

SUBJECT: International Youth Library.

(1) Some time ago the undersigned proposed that the International Children's Book Exhibition be turned into a permanent International Youth Library. The German as well as the foreign press have given this idea an enthusiastic reception, and the principal cities of the American, British, and French zones of occupation have offered to be the site of such a library. There have even been two offers from the Soviet authorities. On 28 March, 1947, the chief of the ICD decided to found such an International Youth Library under American auspices, and invited the undersigned, who has been in charge of the International Children's Books Exhibition since its inception, to present a plan for the formation of an International Youth Library.

(2) The following proposals are submitted herewith:

(a) The International Youth Library is to be supplied with a new basic inventory of books and children's paintings, but all techniques, contacts, connections, questionnaire data, etc., resulting from the International Children's Books Exhibition are of great importance to the library. At the conclusion of the exhibition, to which showings still have been requested from other countries, the books and children's paintings that are still in good condition will be allotted to the library.

(b) The principle of book donations, one of the leading ideas at the International Children's Books Exhibition, shall be retained after its change into a library. It is proposed that all prominent, non-political youth organizations of the various member nations of the United Nations form a committee; that each nation sponsor its own book section and provide a selection of its best books. This method is very important, since it gives responsibility for the maintenance of the national book sections to the young people themselves, a feature which will make the International Youth Library an extraordinary vehicle for understanding among nations. This plan takes precedence over all others. Moreover, it would free the institution from difficulties in foreign exchange. It should be carried on by young people for young people, and could, possibly, permit international exchange of letters and young people themselves.

(c) At least six other places should establish international reading rooms, as branches of the International Youth Library. Books and other materials for these international reading rooms would be supplied by the main library.

(d) A second but equally important area is research in education and psychological studies, which such an international institution ideally could provide as a medium. Co-operation with the universities is of great importance.

(e) A list of youth organizations in the various countries being considered for this collaboration will be submitted in the next few weeks. These organizations will be requested by letter to co-operate in donating books and children's paintings.

(f) Accompanying this request will be a prospectus containing a detailed explanation of the origin and aims of the International Youth Library.

(g) At the same time, the idea of an International Youth Library should be introduced to the public at a press conference.

(h) All departments of Information Control Division and its personnel as, indeed, all members of the occupation authority, should be instructed to contribute any assistance possible.

(i) It is requested that the plan hereby set forth be examined and accepted as soon as possible so that it may be put into effect with the utmost speed.

(j) The undersigned will be available for further information and discussion. Once again let it be emphasized that the founding of such an International Youth Library is a significant contribution to international understanding and to the maintenance of peace.

Jella Lepman

Adviser for Women's and Youth's Affairs

[85]

This piece of writing, which went to the Rockefeller Foundation in similar form, is still a source of great pride to me today. I will even dare to say that the proposals made there would be preferable by far to the present status of the institution. It was based on true internationalism and would not tolerate any false principles calling themselves by the same name. I know that even in the pre-Hitler era international projects were inclined to become fatally Germanicized, though they might still bear the international shield. A disastrous path, but I am afraid it is one we still have not learned any better to avoid . . .

Now matters took their prescribed course. Part of the regular routine was a letter every few months from an American army office directed to 'Allied Personnel', terminating our employment. At first this threat worried us, for whether one was English, French, or stateless (those who had escaped Hitler's wrath), all held important positions. We had been hired because of special abilities, and now we were forced to work with the Sword of Damocles hanging over our heads.

One time I received three different communications by the same post: A commendation from the general on the success of the exhibitions; a letter from personnel giving me notice, 'as the addressee does not hold an American passport,' and confirmation from the Division of my appointment as managing editor of *Heute*.

A measles-like attack of chauvinism obviously had infected some employee of the Pentagon and infested others, causing a rash of termination notices to hit people periodically. Eventually we became immune, and could laugh at them. But sometimes one of us, on impulse and aware of his real worth, would turn in his own letter of termination. It would be returned promptly, stamped 'Rejected.'

v

Sometimes snowdrop blossoms or other signs of spring venture into the light of day as early as January. One morning one of those signs came to me in the form of a letter from the Rockefeller Foundation. It invited me to the United States for a lecture tour, speaking on international understanding through children's books, for a period of several months. The words danced before my eyes. As once before at headquarters, I waved my letter joyfully over the heads of my colleagues, and few of them could hide their envy.

Armed with vaccination papers, travel orders, letters of introduction and flight luggage, I stood in the Munich-Riem air terminal on April 7, 1948. Overhead I noticed a huge eagle stretching its wings, and I could see where a welder had obliterated the swastika. But even that could not destroy my good humour! Since I was the first passenger to fly direct from Munich to New York via American Airways (formerly it was possible to go to America only from Frankfurt, and military planes had handled the traffic from Munich to Frankfurt), the press had turned out in force.

A German journalist asked me, 'Will you be travelling alone?'

'Indeed not,' I replied. 'Thousands of children starving for books are flying along with me . . .'

The flight took nineteen hours, a record time then. My first sight of the ocean, however, was not until we'd reached Newfoundland. And I must confess that I am glad jets weren't being used then, for the transition from the ruination of Germany to the skyscraper land of New York would have been too sudden for me to bear.

[87]

It was love at first sight when I saw New York. And Manhattan at night – it looked like a city out of *A Thousand and One Nights!* I forgot all about sleep in the excitement of reading from this open book of fairy tales. The following morning two cups of strong, hot coffee in a drug store had to make up for it.

Then I set out for Rockefeller Center, mindful of the good advice my American co-workers had given me: 'You can walk anywhere freely when the green traffic light shines. But be careful, red means danger!' (This was a time when there were no traffic lights at all in the ruined cities of Germany.) Also I'd been told, 'Don't expect to see the names of philosophers and poets on street signs. You'll have to be content with mere numbers.'

An elevator shot me up to the 55th floor of the imposing building, and I knocked at the door of Professor Havighurst. Both the view of Manhattan from his office and the programme that had been mapped out for me took my breath away. There were to be contacts with youth organizations, librarians and book publishers, and I would have to find a sponsor for my as yet un-born child, the International Youth Library. Also, there was the matter of rounding up a collection of books for children and young people, gramophone records, children's paintings, films, all, so to speak, as handouts. Most important, I was to keep a sharp look-out for millionaires eager to sink their money into the International Youth Library. I hope nobody blames me for feeling wobbly.

Still quite weak in the knees, I set out to visit the new York field office where General McClure had been transferred and was assigned as chief. He gave me a red-carpet welcome, and at once got down to business.

'How many crates should I expect to have ready to ship your booty home?' he asked. And I felt dazed all over again. . .

St Louis next, where I plunged into the thick of my first American conference, this one sponsored by the American Association of Childhood Education. The affair was most lavish, with more than 2,000 persons in attendance, and most of these were women in bright flowered hats and wearing bouquets of orchids on their lapels. All age groups were present, and it seemed that everybody knew each other. A spirit of zeal and enterprise pervaded the air. And added to all this, their knowledgeability of the subject constantly amazed me.

Lectures and work groups dealt with such topics as co-operation between home and school, legislation for children and young people, neighbourhood aid, and other vital modern questions. The group I was assigned to tackled children's literature, and here I had the opportunity to speak about my special interest. I was filled with fire and others were, too, so much that the group chairman brought out the fire extinguishers. 'What exactly do you want us to do?' she asked. I explained my ideas to them and they concurred. My little seed of understanding through children's books had taken root.

At night these astonishing women, many of them degree-winners in the academic world, blossomed out into elegant women of the world. They glided about in long evening gowns made in all the colours of the rainbow, with bouquets of orchids in their *décolletages*. At the close of the evening they sang the Association song with all the power of their lungs:

> '*Everywhere, everywhere, children tonight,*
> *Everywhere, everywhere, children tonight,*
> *Children who hold in their hearts, minds, and hands,*
> *Promise of freedom and joy in all lands.*
> *Give them our help, as with banner unfurled,*
> *Children today make tomorrow's One World.*
> *Everywhere, everywhere, children tonight,*
> *Everywhere, everywhere, children tonight.*'

The words easily could have been adapted to a song equally as appropriate:

'Nowhere, nowhere, children tonight!'

For not a child was to be seen in the festive, candle-lit room.

I met my first American children in St Louis, in the public library, where a good-natured Negro librarian sat surrounded by cheerful Negro children as she told them the story of Snow White. Sitting on a bench beside one of the little girls, I asked her to draw me a picture of Snow White. She did at once – a Snow White as black as the ace of spades.

I flew on to the headquarters of the American Library Association in Chicago, little knowing what this meeting would mean for me. Chicago – I was frightened of this city, with its slaughter-houses, gangsters, street fights. But before I knew it I was standing in front of Marshall Field's immense department store, with twenty minutes to spare before my appointment. It was my first glimpse into an American department store, and it enthralled me.

Inside, the advent of spring was visible everywhere the eye looked. Pastel colours covered everything, and cascades of chiffon plunged like waterfalls over plastic rocks. A riot of colour greeted me in the millinery department, and a headpiece crowned with flowers nodded to me from its stand. Suddenly there seemed to be the scent of hay in the air, and cowbells ringing – in Marshall Field's department store! Before I realized what I was doing, I was seated before a mirror and a stylish salesgirl was placing a miniature meadow on my head. A French model, it was sinfully expensive, but the flowers were planted firmly on my head and there they remained. The hat proved its worth the moment I walked through the venerable doors of the American Library Association – the A.L.A. – and it became my good luck charm for the rest of the trip.

Mildred Batchelder, executive secretary of the Division of Libraries for Children and Young People, greeted me with open arms, for we had heard a great deal about each other for a long time.

'What a lovely little hat,' she cried.

'I hope you don't have hay fever,' I said, and we both laughed.

I believe, of course, in the good fairy, and knew at once that I had found one in the A.L.A. The International Youth Library could never have acquired the recognition and influence it needed to achieve its goals had it not been for the A.L.A. True to the spirit of fairyland, the A.L.A. was not only willing but ready to act as sponsor for the future International Youth Library.

How different was the position of the library in English speaking countries from what it was in most of Europe began to come clear to me. Here the library was not a dry place for the collection of books, but a living centre for many varied events, and an information bureau for all kinds of questions. Also, everywhere I went there was a special section set aside for the young.

The importance America placed on libraries was reflected in the way librarians were educated, with library schools affiliated with universities. There was a special training programme for children's librarians, and its many-sidedness attracted a lot of young people. These were not dusty old librarians using dusty old library methods. Mentally already I was working out an exchange deal with them, and I was sure who would get the better of the bargain.

With some trepidation I went out to the University of Chicago campus to deliver a lecture. To my relief, I was met by Professor Havighurst, who was a member of both the University of Chicago and the Rockefeller Foundation. On the platform I began presenting the picture of a new world to the professors and students, a world where children's books would be the finest envoys a nation could have. And the focal point would be the first International Youth Library, located in Munich.

A wild discussion broke out immediately. One professor jumped to his feet and cried, 'International understanding through children's books is one thing, and so is the plan for an institution to promote this idea. But why establish such a library in Germany? Europe, certainly, but Germany – after all we've gone through, no!' There was an outburst of applause and then new speakers followed along this line, phrasing the same question.

How easily could I understand their objection. And it was true, many other countries had offered to take the library. But there was no doubt in my mind that Germany's children needed this institution more than all the others. So did German librarians, publishers, and the educators who had been wearing the blinkers imposed by Hitler for twelve years. An International Youth Library such as ours could become a model for the rebuilding of Germany's entire library system. Nowhere could its influence be greater than there. I appealed at last to my audience: 'Even if your prejudices are partly justified, please try to overcome them. The most important thing is to give the children of Germany another chance.'

The reaction that followed was one that never fails to surprise visitors to the United States, not stiff opposition and insistence on hardened opinion, but a straightforward, 'All right, you have convinced us. Now tell us what we can do.' This was the American motto.

Almost at once the University of Chicago formed a committee for the future International Youth Library, and before its work was finished had made valuable contributions towards its construction.

Then the great moment came when I visited the Pentagon. Many of my friends from headquarters in Germany were sitting there now, not at makeshift desks or in requisitioned rooms. They greeted me and gave me coffee. The entire Pentagon, of which secretly I'd been afraid, turned out to be like a round-the-clock restaurant, gigantic and cheerful.

I hope the Russians do not draw any false conclusions from that. After all, these people in the Pentagon had been children once, all of them, and hadn't forgotten their children's books. As a matter of fact, I heard two VIPs devotedly recite nursery rhymes while seated at their executive desks.

Of course we also drew up a plan of strategy for the International Youth Library. Not all strategic plans aim at international unity, as this one did. I was almost sorry when, much to my surprise, I found my way out of the labyrinth of the Pentagon.

Up until then the most I had seen of New York was my hotel and Rockefeller Center. Travel schedules inevitably have a way of running out of hand, and mine certainly was no exception. Even later on I managed only to see that part of the city that was on my official schedule. This included the Museum of Modern Art, where I was more captivated by the art classes for children than I was by all the famous old masters.

The museum's director of education programmes, Victor d' Amico, himself a fine artist, led me to the children working at their easels. There they stood, many of them of pre-kindergarten age, wielding their brushes in beautiful free-form movements. They threw colours on their paper, on their faces, on their smocks – it was an orgy of paint. No one bothered them and no one bullied them with 'No, you can't do that!' They were left alone to paint away to their heart's content.

Many of them took for their subject the city itself. They turned the pages of New York like a book of pictures, discovering hundreds of things an adult never sees. If anyone peered over their shoulders they were unaware of it. Once finished, they scarcely gave their picture another thought. They had painted it out of their deepest selves and laughed in excitement. They knew nothing about Freud and his teachings, these happy American children. But in my mind's eye I couldn't help but see Germany's children and all that weighed upon them, whether they knew it or not. Already I was adding a new wing to my castle in the air – an art studio for children.

Two huge stone lions stood guard over the magnificent New York Public Library, and it was apparent that these were 'happy lions'. In one room I actually came upon an International Youth Library on a reduced scale. Immigrant children – small Italians,

Poles, and Czechs – sought relief from their homesickness here in books and pictures from their native lands.

Everywhere I was swamped with questions, all seeming to spring from a deep hunger to know rather than from mere curiosity. A meeting I had with a children's book publisher was striking proof of this. What a hardy mixture of ideals and plain common sense! Here, books for children had long ceased to be regarded as the stepchild of literature, which so often was the case in old Europe. In America children's books had marched to the front rank. And don't imagine that publishers here waited for a writer to appear with a manuscript under his arm. No, they trained such writers quite deliberately, even if sometimes too deliberately. This also was true for the new-style 'information book', which offered a world of factual knowledge even to the very young. Both the large and small Golden Book series made history, not just by shooting into the blue, but by aiming straight on target. Bright, capable women were employed as readers of children's books, and they often discovered real talent by a kind of sixth sense. The time was right and they were anxious to establish contact with postwar Europe as it rose from the ashes. Evidencing the Christmas spirit as early as summer, they built a pyramid of hundreds of the best American children's books, as a contribution to the International Youth Library. I could hear the children's excited cries already.

An evening I shall never forget: dinner at Eleanor Roosevelt's home in Washington Square. Outside the door there was a small metal plate with her name engraved in plain letters. Her personal secretary and friend for many years, Miss Thompson, met me at the door. It seemed, she told me, that Mrs Roosevelt's meeting with the UNO Human Rights Committee was running into overtime again. She invited me in and I waited.

Ten minutes later Eleanor Roosevelt hurried through the door carrying a briefcase like any other working woman. Ice-cold drinks were served, and we enjoyed the refreshing ritual.

Left: Jella Lepman wearing a uniform of the American Army in Berlin, at the opening of the International Children's Exhibition, 1946.

Right: Self-portrait of Daniel Otake, aged nine, from the 1952 exhibition of children's self-portraits 'Ich Selbst – Myself – Moi Même'.

Left: Jella Lepman with the *Heute* editorial staff, 1947.

Right: The cover of the *American Library Association Bulletin* from February 1950, showing the villa at Kaulbach Straße 11a, residence of the International Youth Library from 1949–83.

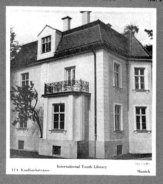

AMERICAN LIBRARY ASSOCIATION

A|A *Bulletin*

Vol. 44 · FEBRUARY · 1950 · No. 2

International Youth Library

11A Kaulbachstrasse   Munich

1950 ANNUAL CONFERENCE · CLEVELAND · JULY 16-22

A poster advertising the first exhibition of the International
Youth Library in Munich, 1949. Self-portrait of a Danish girl, aged seven.

Left: Picture book hour with Jella Lepman, around 1950.

Above: Jella Lepman observing a session of the Young People's United Nations, around 1954. Photograph: Hans Schürer.

Above: Jella Lepman and Erich Kästner (far right) as part of the audience in a lesson at the International Youth Library, around 1950.

Right: Young readers in the International Youth Library, around 1950.

Photograph: Inge Loeffler.

The children are introduced to American books, 1952. Photograph: Inge Loeffler.

Above: Jella Lepman inaugurates the exhibition 'Ich Selbst – Myself – Moi Même', Munich, 1952. **Below:** Children painting on easels in the garden of the International Youth Library, summer 1952. Photograph: Hans Schürer.

Left: The interior of the Book Mobil of the International Youth Library, which made its first journey in 1956.

Below: The 'Book Castle', the medieval Schloss Blutenburg, home to the International Youth Library since 1983.

Surrounding us was lovely antique furniture. On the walls hung various photographs of the Roosevelt family among fine paintings of the old masters. It was a warm, patrician home, the air full of memories and yet at the same time thoroughly contemporary. The mistress of the house carved the roast with skill. Nowhere was there a trace of awkwardness. Mrs Roosevelt and her Negro maid exchanged understanding glances. It was just how I imagined it would be.

Mrs Roosevelt asked me to tell her about the experiences I had had on my missionary travels, and the shrewd and witty comments she made showed her grasp of the possibilities and obstacles in store for us. Suddenly she said, 'I'll send a personal cable to General Lucius Clay in Berlin and ask him to help you with your project.' I was so pleased I almost dropped my fork.

The cable was sent off the next morning, and General Clay replied the following day. He thanked Eleanor Roosevelt for her interest in building an International Youth Library in Germany and assured her of his support.

That night Mrs Roosevelt wrote about our meeting in her daily column, 'My Diary,' which was read by millions throughout the country. The column went like this:

May 27, 1948
FOOD FOR THOUGHT

'I have just been talking to a most interesting woman who has done one of those remarkably unselfish things which very few people manage to make themselves do. Having lost in Germany all that made life worth living, she escaped to England, and then, after the war, went back on a British passport. In spite of thinking that she could not bear to work with the Germans, she found herself working to try to feed the children – not only food for their tummies but food for their minds.

'She put on the International Book Fair, where children came to look at books as at some curious, wonderful thing. They queued and stood for hours to sit down at a library table and look at a picture book. I met this woman when I was in Germany in 1946, and now she is here and getting support and books for her children's libraries over there.

'Without books how can the minds of the small German children be opened to new ideas? How can the minds of the older children be changed, so they will understand there are other points of view besides those they were taught under Hitler?

'... Yes, the time has come to help the German children as well as the other children of Europe. But don't forget to send books as well as food. We must not let the children grow up again into young Nazis and Fascists, so we have to give them food for thought?'

It is hard to believe the effect such an article can have. The telephone in my hotel room began ringing without letup. Messengers flitted in and out with packages, and telegrams were waiting for me at the breakfast table. Reporters begged for interviews. 'The Voice of America' and other radio programmes and stations fought to have me speak on their shows. Thank heaven, I thought – General McClure was not getting his crates ready for nothing!

At the same time my campaign for an International Youth Library was going on, the clamour of the American presidential campaign was at its peak. The Democrats were fighting for the re-election of President Truman, the Republicans for their candidate, Dewey. One day the National Republican Women's League invited me to dinner. This imposing body filled me with awe, and I had no idea whom to thank for the invitation. I had shared the proverbial 'pot luck' with the most important Democrat, Mrs Roosevelt, and now I was to do the same with the opposition.

The Republicans were perfect hosts, too. I sat next to the charming Mrs Wendell Wilkie and we discussed her husband's book, *One World*. We were sure he would have placed no less importance on the idea of 'One Children's World.'

Then the mysterious man appeared whom obviously I had to thank for the invitation – Congressman Everett M. Dirksen, the night's guest of honour. We had met on one of his trips to Germany. His appetite for knowledge had struck me as amazing. Even that night he began assaulting me with questions. Was my project advancing? What response was I getting in the United States? Then the chairman, Mrs Bacon, tugged him gently by the sleeve – a crowded auditorium was waiting to hear him speak.

I had never heard a congressman speak before a body of the electorate. It was better by far than a first night at the theatre. The walls themselves trembled from the ovation the audience gave the star of the evening.

Another high point of my trip was the day I met Frederic D. Melcher, who inaugurated the Caldecott and Newbery medals, the highest award given to American children's books. He looked exactly the way one would picture a patron of children's books, and he had energy enough for an entire organization.

My farewell to New York was marked by a sunset that looked like an immense firework display. Mrs Wilkie saw me off on the *Mauretania* with confident words of encouragement – 'One children's world . . .'

vi

The ocean expanse between America and Europe seemed boundless. When I finally got to Munich bad news at once started raining down. Overnight the currency reform had gone into effect, wiping away the American military government's emergency funds. We were as poor as church mice, which struck me, having just returned from the States, as particularly incredible. Many cultural construction projects became, suddenly, so many castles in the air. I had every reason to feel shaky. The plan for the International Youth Library would have been carried away with all the others by this tidal wave, had it not been for Eleanor Roosevelt's cable to General Clay.

So it won a reprieve, but even at that ran the risk of starving to death. We were assigned two small offices in the courthouse of the American military government. It was not uncommon to meet criminals in the corridors, handcuffed, of course. In addition, the American personnel office issued regular orders every weekend stating that because of the shortage in funds, all employees would have to be summarily dismissed. It was not as though we had an enormous staff. Besides my secretary, who herself carried out half a dozen jobs, the only other person we had was a handy man. Each time such an order came through, I tried to keep it secret from whomever it threatened, then I would make my painful way to the personnel officer to explain the disastrous impression such high-handed measures made. Luckily, I wasn't the only one to adopt that tack. The warning decrees would be rescinded and the matter suspended indefinitely.

Pushing my luck, I went in search of a building. I drove up and down Munich's bombed streets in a jeep. One prospect after another fell through, for I had rather specific ideas about my dream house. Then one day I fell head over heels in love. The cause of this about-face was a building that even amidst the ruins appeared charming. It was one of those small city mansions built in Kaulbachstrasse towards the end of the nineteenth century, surrounded by a large, neglected garden where birds sang.

I had no idea who owned the house, or whether it was occupied in spite of its bomb damage. But to myself I said, 'Yes!' loud and clear, and have never regretted it.

The authorities are a necessary part of the body politic – the backbone, so to speak – but all the same there were many times when I could have done without them. It was a vicious circle. At that time the American officials didn't want to undertake anything without including the Germans. Sometimes that was a mistake. The Germans could not undertake anything. That, simply, was a fact of occupation. The lawful owner of the building on Kaulbachstrasse was the Bavarian ministry of culture; therefore, the landlord was the well-known minister of culture, Herr Hundhammer. That dignified gentleman had no idea that the basement of the building was, in fact, occupied, by some people making cosmetics there. The American military government stepped in and offered the future Institute of Beauty space in an old barracks. Then the building was vacated.

I'm sure that George Bernard Shaw could have written a satire on all that happened next, although at the time it seemed more like a tragi-comedy to me. So much was still up in the air – you might say the whole house was up in the air. There was only one thing possible to do, and that was to ignore everything and work for the best.

And that is what I did. Sitting at my desk until midnight with my overworked secretary, drawing up budgets (in case the Rockefeller Foundation really came through), designing ground plans (in case the ministry of culture said 'Yes'), and drawing up a work schedule (in case the world was still intact by then). But of course the world would not end as long as one believed firmly in his cause and did not let anyone or anything deflect him from his goal.

Herr Hundhammer was a man of principles who had been thrown into a concentration camp by the Nazis. Now he tugged at his famous beard. It seemed to him that the time was not yet ripe for my international organization. According to him, there were more pressing things to be done closer to home. His state secretary, Dr Dieter Sattler, was a cultured man with a conciliatory nature and many times he jumped into the swirl when the minister and I churned up rough seas. Looking back, I should feel conscience-stricken when I remember the curse I hurled at the minister at the close of this interview. 'Generations of children will curse you if you keep us from building an International Youth Library!' I cried. He paled visibly, and suddenly I realized the extent of my arrogance. Here was a man struggling with a conflict within himself, that, in spite of everything, did him justice. I reached out my hand for his, hoping we could forgive each other, and he took it. The next day a letter arrived giving us permission to use the building.

That, in short story form, is how the International Youth Library came to be on Kaulbachstrasse. Really it is a novel of many chapters stretching over almost a year.

Germany had undergone a metamorphosis with the currency reform. Things one formerly would hardly have dared dream about suddenly were available. The occupation dollar lost its power, and the black market its justification. People's eyes brightened with hope, though they themselves might not be able to enter the paradise of delicatessens, perfumeries, and automobile showrooms right away. But soon they could! For the first time they were feeling once more solid ground under their feet. The tiredness vanished from their faces, and a boundless urge to get out from under seized everyone.

This was the curtain raiser on the second postwar phase of

German recovery, and to the third, later to be called 'The German miracle'. Responsibility for state and municipal governments, agriculture, and industry, was passed over into German hands in double-quick time. The denazification programme began to show its inadequacies. Judges, doctors, civil servants, college professors, librarians, and teachers who were supposedly purified by this cleansing agent, resumed their old places and picked up where they had left off. Naturally they were careful of saying in public whether they hated Hitler for anything more than the humiliation of losing the war, or whether they lamented the loss of his 'Thousand-year Reich'.

Those most endangered, however, were the children, who often had no home, were without childhood, and faced a future helplessly at the mercy of the adult world. When would at least some of them find refuge in the rooms of the International Youth Library? Climbing over rubble and ruins I urged the construction workers to hurry, but they needed no urging at all.

In the meantime, our offices had been moved into other emergency quarters, this time in one of the most beautiful structures in Munich, the feudal *Prinz Carl Palais*. Mussolini had stayed there once on the occasion of Chamberlain's historic 'Peace in our time' mission. We were walking over the ground of modern history. Our team was ensconced in rooms with high ceilings and huge windows and double doors. Unfortunately, it was practically heatless. So we wore three sweaters and kept warm by working. We thought at last the worst was behind us, but what a mistake that was!

The dark forces of international politics began edging closer to war than to peace in the autumn of 1948. The Munich military post gave instructions which read: 'Should it become necessary because of local disruptions or an uprising of the population, American civilians are ordered to gather at the following assembly points . . . *Equipment:* the following articles should be brought to the assembly point —

1. One piece of hand luggage per person.
2. Two wool blankets per person.
3. One article of warm underclothing.

Of course there was no question of the Germans revolting. That reference was a euphemism for war. It was madness. We had scarcely begun disentangling ourselves from the chaos of the last war, and already we were thinking of the next.

No, I refused to prepare for the next war. From that I wouldn't want to be saved.

Some people are born to assume responsibility, to make order out of confusion, to drive points of law into the earth like pillars. Such a personality was the impressive lawyer Dr Franz Stadelmayer, the first acting mayor of Munich. Though he declared with disarming frankness that he knew nothing about children's books except those he read as a boy, he founded a Society of Friends of the International Youth Library, an organization which was a pre-requisite at the local level to get a Rockefeller grant.

He managed to bring this off quite easily. Each member was picked as an uncommitted individual, not as a representative of any faction. These 'friends' were Josef Söhngen, a prominent bookseller and member of the resistance, who was named treasurer of an empty treasury; Dr Anton Fingerle, educator and pioneer in German-American co-operative projects; Dr Grassel, an advocate of youth exchange programmes; the writer Luiselotte Enderle, and Dr Hildegard Brücher, who will appear again later. Our staunchest 'friend' was Dr Walter Gerlach, a physics professor and three times chancellor of Munich University. With his endowment fund for studies, he was later a regular visitor to the International Youth Library.

A million visitors had seen the Exhibition. It was hard to believe that the books were still in decent condition. Children had looked at them, read them, and hugged them to their hearts. The charming Captain Tanguy wrote me a disappointed letter from the French zone, saying, '. . . many books, I am afraid, have dog-

[102]

eared or torn pages . . .' I tried to ease his mind by writing, 'Can anything better happen to books than for them to be read to pieces?'

Once more I spent late hours corresponding with our loyal and trusted friends, whose numbers had grown considerably. After all, could publishers ask for a better display window than the International Youth Library?

'And how do you plan to catalogue?' professional people began asking me. 'Of course you'll be using the Prussian instructions.' They were convinced that there was no other classification system in the world more perfect than theirs. Little did I know how in the future this subject would drive me almost to the point of crying out for a sedative.

Throughout the world's national and international libraries the Dewey decimal system was preferred, and the system had been recognized internationally for years. Unfortunately, Mr Dewey had not forseen the International Youth Library with its books in many languages. Since this high priest of cataloguing no longer was among us, obviously we had to adjust his work and adapt his system to our needs. I sat down at the elegant baroque desk of the *Prinz Carl Palais*, pulled a wool blanket over my knees, and wrote to the American Library Association, asking them to send us an expert to act as a consultant. In the meantime, we began a straightforward listing of titles, with only the language barrier to skirt round.

Also we read each book, not the normal procedure that it would seem. For not everybody who catalogues books loves them and reads them, too. This was a fact that didn't dawn on me until later.

As we busied ourselves with these details, the children who later would be our guests wandered around in the streets and among the building sites. I thought: Why not hold story hours for them? However, I hadn't reckoned on my host, if I may so describe Count Podewils, the custodian of the *Prinz Carl Palais*. He and his officials closed ranks against an 'invasion of children'. Never would the dirty shoes of children defile the floors of the *Prinz*

Carl Palais. Even a suggestion that they might leave their shoes at the door had no effect.

The children had further competition in the form of a famous collection of antique Greek vases. Count Podewils, who was no bureaucrat really, but a poet, tried over and over to explain to me – ignoramus that I obviously was – how unique this miraculously preserved collection of vases was.

I failed to see how children who loved books could behave like vandals, so I suggested simply locking the doors on these sacred relics. 'That is just what would tempt them most, locked doors,' the count said, and I was stymied.

Nowadays, whenever I happen to look at the noble vases on exhibit in the hall of the *Prinz Carl Palais*, it is clear to me how audacious my demands were. But at the time, to the count's horror, I shouted, 'Believe me, living children are more important than dead vases.' However, he held his ground and the children remained barred.

His essential generosity was evidenced later, when he opened the banquet hall of the *Prinz Carl Palais* to the Christmas parties for the children.

The long-awaited cable arrived in the spring of 1949. It read: ROCKEFELLER FOUNDATION APPROVES A TWO-YEAR GRANT OF $22,000 FOR THE ESTABLISHMENT OF AN INTERNATIONAL YOUTH LIBRARY IN MUNICH.

'Hurrah!' we all shouted, and felt that we had leaped over the biggest hurdle.

The *Prinz Carl Palais* was an ice palace no longer. The spring sun streamed through the windows and over Munich lay that deep blue sky that makes it the loveliest of all German cities. The skeleton of the house in the Kaulbachstrasse was finished, and often I would sit on a little stairway leading down into the garden and give myself over to the pleasures of anticipation, the sweetest kind of joy.

One brilliant day in midsummer the expert sent by the American Library Association, Margaret Scoggin, appeared, a happy event for our expanding organization. She literally rolled up her sleeves and immediately set to work.

As fate would have it, Würzburg elected the first president of our organization as its mayor, a blow to our infant venture because he would now have to leave us. Then one day we were paid a visit by Dr Heiner Lades, the rising young chairman of the Bavarian Youth Association. He came, saw, and conquered – to remain our new president. And I will always remember how well he did by his adopted child.

Staffing our Foreign Legion was a ticklish business. Hardly any applicants possessed the necessary qualifications. Adolf Hitler had cut off Germany and its librarians from the free world so thoroughly, it had made it difficult for them to learn foreign languages. The knowledge of French some of them had acquired during the German occupation of Paris was, at most, a dubious asset.

There also was the question of international children's literature. The masterpieces had all been burned, and for twelve years children's books from the free world had been banned from Germany. Open-access libraries, taken for granted elsewhere, were regarded with suspicion here. The modern idea of a library for young people which was an open house for children's books was practically unheard of. And so was the idea of training children's librarians in a college affiliated with a university.

It was a miracle that in spite of all this a staff was assembled, headed by the imaginative and gifted Dorothea Lauruschkus. We plunged feverishly into preparations, often stumbling over each other in our excitement.

It was a surprise to us to see the 14th of September, 1949, dawn like any other day. To us, it seemed that all the new-cast bells in Munich should have boomed out in rejoicing.

Opening ceremonies, like birth and death, follow a prescribed pattern of ritual. First the well-meant or ill-meant speeches are made, then the most prominent person present cuts the ribbon. No one had thought of a ribbon, though, or a bottle of champagne as for launching a ship, but that didn't seem to bother the guests streaming into the rooms. We had no postwar *Who's Who*, but we might have started one then. The many languages being spoken sounded like the tower of Babel, but people managed to make themselves understood. And not to be overlooked was the delegation of children who were present.

These children gave the opening ceremony its deepest significance. They read aloud from their favourite books in the original language. An American boy chose *Ferdinand the Bull*; a Swedish girl, *The Wonderful Adventures of Little Nils Holgersson*; a little Italian boy, *Pinocchio*; a Swiss girl, *Heidi*; a German boy – what else – *Emil and the Detectives*, and a French child read from *Babar the Elephant*. They sang and played music, laughed and danced, and half the world heard all this over the radio.

In the afternoon, the house finally was given over to the children. They formed a procession, paid their respects to their favourite books, and spelled out the foreign titles. In the United States they call such an affair as ours that day a 'housewarming', and that is exactly what it was. The stone walls warmed, books and children's paintings radiated a secret life. Many good spirits marched in, and a few less good stole in with them, but we took no notice of them . . .

Any party without a hangover is hardly worth the name. Our hangover was in the realization that we had opened our doors with nothing but a mere catalogue of titles. After long discussions with our expert from America, we had decided to start with a catalogue of authors and illustrators and not try to systematize the cataloguing for a couple of years. Since we were the first big international youth library on either side of the ocean, we wanted to get over the worst part first.

The 'brains' of the German library field, however, greeted our decision with cries of anguish, since cataloguing was their hobby-horse. And when they saw the variety of activities the library offered, they began spreading the word around that this was not a library at all, but a circus.

Nevertheless, hordes of happy children and adults steamed into the circus tent. The autumn wind whistled through the streets, spinning colourful leaves along the walks leading to our entrance. The house was warm and cheerful, and the cloak room attendant, Frau Beck, greeted each visitor who came in. She soon observed how few were the warm coats hanging on the hooks, and shoes that were weird creations made out of cardboard. We sent word of this to our friends in the beautiful land of America, and before Christmas was over there no longer were hooks enough to hold the duffle coats sent from overseas.

It was still impossible to separate cultural and social questions in postwar Germany. Children without soap cannot keep their hands clean. Children in cheap cotton dresses in winter time shiver in the cold. Homeless children look like tramps. And what child can concentrate on a book when his little stomach is growling?

What good was the most organized library programme if these basic human problems were not faced? In those days children's librarians wrestled with problems they were never trained in school to solve. This meant a challenge for many, while others resented the additional burden.

'Tell me,' a university professor from Ann Arbor asked, 'how can Nazi parents give birth to children such as these?'

'The fact,' I replied, 'is that every child is the start of a new life. That's the whole secret.'

Actually these children absorbed anything new with remarkable *naïveté*. They were burning up with curiosity. Yet it was rare when they overstepped the limits that were laid down. Their self-control was at once sad but helpful to us. They would not put up with dirty fingernails or running noses in themselves or others. Anyone who owned a Sunday suit – either a new one or one he'd been wearing for a time – would don it for his library visit and explain, 'It's always Sunday when I come here.' I remembered my little girl's outburst in Berlin, 'Yes, this must be peace!' It was like a refrain.

Many were the forbidding predictions that swamped us. 'The children might steal half the books,' some prophets said. We knew we were in the spotlight. The question as to whether future children's librarians in Germany would adopt the open-shelf concept depended almost entirely on us. And our books did look tempting in their transparent coverings.

But these doom-saying prophets were wrong. Hardly a single book disappeared or was lost. We needed only to tell these children that friends from all over the world had sent them these books, and they were so swept up by the thought that they wanted to hear it repeated again and again.

Occasionally, however, a child could not bear to give up a story he'd begun and he would smuggle the book home under his sweater. For this, there was a shelf in a corner of the library where the book could be returned without anyone being the wiser.

The picture-book room was an ideal place to conduct experiments. Children of all age groups sat there, even those of preschool age. These picture-books vaulted over the language barrier and struck the child's memory easily and directly. Their world spoke of what all children knew: mother and father, brother and sister, dog, cat, the apple tree or palm tree outside the front door, sun, moon, and stars; the birthday cake made of wheat, maize or soya flour, a ball to play with; the swings and merry-go-rounds of the fair. We had a 'United Nations of Children' right in front of our eyes, and all we had to do was follow their example.

The children drinking in the red, yellow, and green illustrations were filled with delight; flowers in the picture books were their own birthday bouquets; the market place and pointed gables enclosing it became a part of their ruined villages. They pulled their own little chair to the table with the laughing family of bears. And, too, this was their first encounter with foreign languages.

Their gibberish was like a children's Esperanto. These books were silent educators, secret ambassadors from the nations of their origin. Jean de Brunhoff's *Babar the Elephant* showed the children more about the Frenchman's way of thinking than a stack of confusing history books would later. Virginia Lee Burton's *The Little House* was a special ambassador from America. There the house stood on a green meadow, and irresistably the concrete of the city spreading around it. Then what happens? Two men load the little house on a truck and drive it out to another green meadow. On its way, its windows smile at the children happily, as though to say: 'You see, even this works out.'

Picture-books depict the most lovable sides of foreign countries. No doubt such books also are the first educational ones a child has. Whole new areas were opening up in this field, and suddenly there were information books – a rather clumsy nomenclature, but their contents were breathtaking. Every subject under the sun was covered: natural science, technology, art, literature, even religion and history. These picture books broke through the confines of the genre and attracted an entirely new readership. The small and large Golden Books appeared in America. In Paris, Paul Faucher at Flammarion got together a team of experts and created '*Les albums du père castor.*' The Swiss launched the '*Schweizer Jugendschriftenwerk*' and its originality set a model no other country was able to equal.

The biggest success scored by the children's book room was The Story Hour. Is there anything new under the sun? The ancient art of story-telling had travelled from Europe to America and now come back again over the ocean. No television set, no matter how advanced, would ever replace the magic bond of a tale between the child and the story-teller.

Their faces alive with interest, older children browsed through the shelves where books were arranged according to language, then sub-classified by subject. How thrilling it was to choose a book oneself! We asked ourselves why our young readers shouldn't write reviews of those books themselves. These books spoke directly to them. Surely these children had something to say about the books.

Thus our first experiment, as novel for librarians as for the children. And it gave publishers a chance to hear the opinions of their audience. These reviews, honest and original, were written between 1949 and 1952:

Helmut Bittner: *Tracks in the Snow* (Germany).
'. . . one expects to have the writer knowing a little more about his subject, at least when he's writing a book on skiing. He doesn't even know what a slalom race is . . .' (13-year-old).

Lewis Carroll: *Alice in Wonderland* (England).
'. . . what a silly translation! It spoiled the whole book. I'd rather have my mother do the translating – she's a thousand times better . . .' (10-year-old).

James Curwood: *Neewa the Bear Cub* (America).
'. . . such a sweet book, and good for grown-ups too. I feel like I'm the happy little bear cub all the way through . . .' (8-year-old).

Charles Dickens: *David Copperfield* (England).
'It's good to see that David Copperfield is not pictured as a genius, but as a real person, hard-working and talented, but normal in every other way . . .' (12-year-old).

Kurt Held: *Red Zora* (Switzerland).
'. . . some older people think this book isn't right for us because not all the people in it are good. But that's just being old-fashioned. After all, we're not babies . . .' (13-year-old).

Erich Kästner: *The Flying Classroom* (Germany).
'. . . how nice people can be to each other, and how many things in the world connect with each other! People have no idea . . .' (12-year-old).

Selma Lagerlöf: *The Girl of the Moor Farm* (Sweden).

'. . . what a beautiful book! I've read it twice. No, I wouldn't dare criticize a book like this . . .' (13-year-old).

C. D. Lane: *Three Boys and a Sail Boat* (America).

'. . . even though it's awfully American, it keeps you on the edge of your seat!' (12-year-old).

Munro Leaf: *Ferdinand the Bull* (America).

'. . . Ferdinand was a very funny bull, but you can often find people like him. He likes to be alone, and so do a lot of human beings . . .' (12-year-old).

Astrid Lindgren: *Bill Bergson: Master Detective* (Sweden).

'. . . if you look closely, you'll come across some awful blunders. The gangster just tears up a special delivery letter and throws it in the waste basket without burning it . . . What a fool!' (14-year-old).

Dhan Gopal Mukerji: *Kari the Elephant* (India).

'. . . the elephant is very easy for me to understand since I see him as a person anyway . . .' (13-year-old).

Wilhelm Raabe: *The Black Galley* (Germany).

'. . . pure nonsense, and unbelievable. The girl is so silly she falls down in a faint instead of defending herself . . .' (12-year-old).

Antoine de Saint-Exupéry: *Wind, Sand and Stars* (France).

'. . . it takes a while to get used to the peculiar style, but once you do this book is beautiful. It says what an ordinary person cannot find the words to say himself . . .' (13-year-old).

William Saroyan: *The Human Comedy* (America).

'. . . although the city is typically American, it could just as

well be German. Things are the same all over the world . . .'
(13-year-old).

Book discussion groups were our next experiment, with the
average age of the participants fourteen – mostly pupils from the
higher secondary school grades – and both sexes equally represented. All were volunteers, but not all without ambitions to be radio
stars. Now a 'woman with the broom' myself, I began sweeping
up the inevitable debris of war. Clichés ran rampant about the
Nazi period, about the war, the occupation, about coexistence.
Obviously these were the undenazified views of parents, teachers,
and questionable history books. Not until we came to what these
children themselves thought about these questions did real discussion begin. They were starving for truthful information, for
historical facts, and discussions about the border. They even
offered to wade through foreign books, deciphering them with
the aid of a dictionary. In books from their own country, contemporary history was being treated like the plague.

Paperback books contributed willingly by publishers, though
some expressed doubts, enabled these young critics to read through
a book in two weeks, providing they worked in a group. A young
people's radio programmer approached us, having got wind of a
possible scoop for his station. I was full of doubts about this, for
we were not out to develop radio stars. However, I did give in
finally and accepted this unique opportunity to gain a large number of supporters via the airwaves.

One time a book about refugees came up for discussion. It was
by a German author, and she and her publisher were invited as
guests. The man from the radio station sat among us with his
recording equipment.

As soon as the speaker selected by the young participants gave
a brief report on the book's contents and its themes, hands shot
up in the air. It was my job to moderate, keeping the children in
line. The anxious author had no idea of the storm about to break
over her head.

'Are you a refugee yourself?' one child asked. 'Did you write this book from your own experience?'

The woman's answer was not very convincing.

'I'm a real refugee,' the boy said.

'Me too, me too,' a chorus of young voices cried with emotion. 'You can't fool us.'

The cutting onslaught of errors – imagined and in fact – found in her book were hurled at the author. Then came the dramatic climax.

'Did you ever think of why there are refugees?' somebody said. 'Or about whose fault it is? It's your Hitler's fault, the man you broke into wild rhapsodies about in the children's books you wrote during the war.' And they had quotations at their fingertips. I stood frozen at the microphone. It had never occurred to me that noted authors from the Nazi period already were being prepared for presentation at court once again.

The helpless author was near to tears. Strenuously trying to control her voice, she defended herself. 'I fell victim to Hitler through false idealism. Don't you allow people to see their errors and change?'

'Yes,' they all cried in unison, 'when the change is genuine. But we can't allow them to write books for us so soon again.'

The radio station transmitted the broadcast uncut – the discussion group had survived its acid test.

On another occasion, when the discussion was being taped for later broadcast, the topic was a book that supported the notion of parental authority with absolute Victorian sternness. The young discussion group protested heatedly.

'Never,' they said. 'Our parents have left us with a horrible legacy and we no longer believe you are infallible.'

The youngest and boldest then played his trump card.

'Parents should be done away with altogether,' he cried.

A burst of laughter, in spite of the gravity of the subject, came through the tape and probably saved our necks.

[113]

This time I was summoned to the broadcasting building and there was a general shaking of heads.

'We'll have to erase that part,' the experts declared with pedagogic conviction.

'Erase it? Why?' I said innocently. 'People can speak freely in Germany now.'

This new state of affairs was still strange to them, too new to tamper with. But they relented, and the idea of abolishing parents passed the censor.

'What the International Youth Library really is, is a "university for children",' Erich Kästner said. 'All that's missing here are the bearded professors.' Always on our toes for a good idea, we were proud to recognize the truth of this and it spurred us on to another achievement. We distributed leaflets declaring 'Children's Books Teach Languages. Sign up now for this adventure! English – French – Dutch – Italian – Swedish.'

Enthusiastic students nearly broke down our doors. Some alarmed teachers almost did, too, who saw in our venture 'an attack on the method of teaching languages used in schools.' We calmed them down and asked them to look in later and observe our 'rival undertaking' with their own eyes.

Of course, our advantage lay in our being a small, private circle of students, an inviting atmosphere, and voluntary study. Wherever possible, group leaders came from the language and cultural region being studied. The chief advantage, though, was in the fact that we did not use dusty grammar manuals, but books sent us by the countries themselves as their best offerings. The child's eye would devour the picture and at the same time the words, while the sounds of the words would be absorbed by their ears as the words were spoken aloud. Suddenly one day, completely without their realizing it, the children would begin to speak in a foreign language. Mistakes were made, of course, but the right intonation was got. It wasn't unusual for their zeal to carry over into their schoolwork – and the marks would go up – and sometimes

[114]

down. Our library-circus was too enticing. Parents and teachers wagged threatening fingers, and often enacted a strict ban on the library for their children. The poor sinners would unhappily tell us their plight, and we would comfort them, saying that it was up to them ultimately to have the ban lifted by getting good marks. Anyway, our resourceful Ursula Lessing, the head of the language programme, usually managed to convince the parents to allow the children to attend.

In an attempt to awaken buried artistic talents, a theatre group came next. Who first thought of the idea? In 1950 a group of would-be stars were discussing the project with Erich Kästner. Shakespeare, Kleist, Thornton Wilder, all went by the boards. Suddenly one boy piped up, 'Why not write our own play? Something wholly made for us.' There was resounding applause. Everyone believed that here he had found his calling. Kästner observed in a whisper, 'A writers' collective – what an experiment this will be.'

The response to the idea was tremendous. Of course, an enthusiasm for the sensational had something to do with it, too. It wasn't every day that these young people had a chance to work with an internationally famous author. Fifteen hopeful authors made the grade.

'What will the subject be?' Erich Kästner asked, a mischievous sparkle in his eyes. 'Remember, you'll be writing this play. I have nothing to do with it.'

'No visionary, high-blown stuff,' the most outspoken of the group cried. 'Let's stick to reality.'

'Reality?' their mentor asked. 'What do you mean by reality?'

'Everyday life, of course. *Our* everyday life.'

'Everday life.' the youngest one of the group mumbled. 'We get that all the time. Let's do the opposite. Let's have a fairy tale.'

A storm of abuse broke over the poor boy's head.

'Take your fairy tales back to kindergarten where you belong,' somebody said.

[115]

'Wait a minute. Take it easy,' Erich Kästner broke in. 'Maybe we can meet half-way.'

'But are there any fairy tales left today?' a timid feminine voice said. 'I don't think there are.'

We decided that it would be worth losing a little sleep in order to think over the question of reality versus the fairy tale. Finally it was agreed that we should take as the subject of our play, 'Our search for fairy tales in the big city.'

Collective collaboration in playwriting had its drawbacks. Here sat a group of young people who all were individuals (already amazing for postwar Germany) with violently clashing views. Would a coherent piece of work ever result? 'So what?' they said. 'It would be horrible if we all thought alike, or *had* to think alike.'

What did these young writers discover in their search for fairy tales in the big city? Behind the façade of everyday life lived witches and fairies, Hans in Luck, the Sleeping Beauty, Cinderella. All that was needed was the imagination to recognize them. The writers themselves were drawn into the magic circle while hunting out fairy tales. The world was not empty of enchantment. The marvellous and the terrifying, the chase and the rescue, were everywhere. And fairy tales themselves were nothing more than true experiences concealed in gold, silver, or rags.

Every time the playwrights got together, a new role suggested itself. Before it was over there were fifteen roles, all major ones, for the fifteen members. And Erich Kästner had wisely let them do what they wished, though probably he couldn't restrain an occasional smile. The point demonstrated by the experiment was conclusive: You can't stage a play with nothing but leading roles. Even this lesson, hard as it was to swallow, could be applied to real life. . .

Carl Zuckmayer gave a first reading from his play *Gesang im Feuerofen* (Singing in the Oven) at the IYL, as the library had now come to be familiarly known. There he stood, a tree torn out by its roots by National Socialism and transplanted for years in Vermont. The listeners that day understood the symbolism of his play and went home in a thoughtful mood.

Another time, Alice Herdan-Zuckmayer read from her book, *The Farm in the Green Hills*, which tells the story of how a husband and wife, both writers, lived in exile. They had to stoke their own furnace, carry the wood and feed the chickens. They sat alone in the blizzard, though there were good neighbours, American ones, who helped them out and took them into their own society after the Zuckmayers had been deprived of citizenship in their homeland.

Early one winter afternoon a troop of young girls showed up in the exhibition hall with their teacher. The girls were blind, but nevertheless they moved from picture to picture and listened breathlessly as their sighted companion described each painting. It was thrilling to watch them and to witness the teacher's interpretation of the paintings and the way she used language as though she were fashioning a sculpture. Black and white, red and green, for her, meant more than we would ordinarily suppose.

'The children would like very much to join your library while we're here,' the teacher said to me.

I felt momentary panic. Then I asked the children, 'Which books do you like best?'

'The same as other girls,' a young girl answered. 'Not stories about saints and good children.' These blind girls with their extraordinary capacity for experience, soon became regular visitors.

Publishers all over Germany and abroad began looking forward to our Christmas exhibition, which soon became an annual event. Here the publishers found the latest books of many nations, and it was not only for idealistic rewards that these people came to us in Germany. Literary agencies at first were reluctant to deal with Germany, but now we were bombarded by publishers themselves with suggestions of books to be translated. We became as zealous as missionaries in a savage land. No sooner did a first-rate foreign book fall into our hands, than we argued about which German publisher should have it. Worthwhile copyrights were valuable, and the surest way to raise children's book production out of its doldrums in Germany.

Not all publishers regarded us as their guiding spirits – many thought we were troublesome promoters of inferior and costly foreign books. When they did deign to accept a book which later became a best seller, it wasn't unusual for them to forget to tell us the good news. We would triumphantly add it to our own list of successful achievements.

Unfortunately, we were inexperienced in business. When somebody well-versed in the trade pointed out the unique position we were in to launch an international agency for children's books, we were dismayed. 'What a lucrative sideline!' he cried with eagerness that was almost pathetic. 'You'd be rid of your money worries in no time at all.'

I was doubtful about this. After all, we were a 'charitable' organization. It seemed to us better to give the best books of all nations away for a heavenly reward rather than for an earthly one, thus retaining our freedom of judgment and criticism.

This policy also could be applied in reverse. We encouraged foreign publishers to take up German translation rights even though the choice of books was severely limited. The Nazi régime had left behind a yawning void. We waited in vain for manuscripts to be produced from secret drawers, but no signs of an underground movement in children's books ever emerged – a bitter disappointment.

'Who is the king's daughter who bit into a red apple and fell lifeless to the ground?' (Snow White). 'Who knows the name of that amusing fellow who pulled himself out of the swamp by his own pigtail?' (Münchhausen). 'What young rascal from America has won world fame for his escapades?' (Tom Sawyer). 'Who is the wonderful nursemaid who was blown into the house by a wind?'

(Mary Poppins). 'Who rode her horse over the school house steps?' (Pippi Longstocking).

Book-quiz fever hit the IYL before quizzes were yet popular. German and American children practically sat on top of each other in a crowded room, the way people sit watching a football match. We held up the books and the children shouted out the names and the titles to us. In the course of time our thinly disguised descriptions of characters and books grew more and more ingenious – it became one of my favourite pastimes. One country would win a session today, another one tomorrow. But the most important part of the whole thing was the common discovery that these children, so varied in their backgrounds, knew and loved the same books.

Among the American school children there were always several Negro pupils, who played freely with their classmates. These were the children of members of the occupying forces. There were also other Negro children in postwar Germany who, illegitimate, were not protected by American law. The German radio discussed this subject:

'How can these children help their colour? Sometimes today, when you see little blackamoors in the playgrounds of German cities and towns, you feel as though you're watching a scene from *Struwwelpeter*. Not so long ago even Negro dolls were banned in Germany. But it would be completely wrong to say that the man in the street looks down his nose at these children, who are, after all, half German. Children are much too appealing to bring out such an attitude, and today people are ready to be tolerant.

'Of the 13,000 children whose fathers belong to the American occupation forces in Germany, about 3,000 are coloured. Naturally, most Negro children are found where the Negro troops are stationed – in Munich and Frankfurt, for example. Their way of life is no different from that of any German child. It's strange indeed to hear such a child talking to his playmates in perfect Bavarian or Hessian dialect.

'But it would be wrong to look only at the idyllic side of the

[119]

question. These children present a quite serious problem. Certainly, the largest percentage of coloured children live with their mothers or grandparents, but there are more and more cases where the children have been abandoned because their mothers are afraid of complications. Then these children wind up in municipal or state homes. They are treated there just like their white-skinned contemporaries.

'Sometimes the child's presence prompts the parents to marry. But once an unwed mother has the chance of marrying a white man, the child is looked on as an interloper and every effort is made to get rid of it. Child welfare workers could write volumes on such cases.

'It is interesting that there is a certain call for adopting coloured children by coloured American families. These adoptions are arranged through churches and other religious groups, but sometimes individual German families act as intermediaries. After his release from prison, an SS officer who had served as Hitler's bodyguard explained his motive in marrying the mother of a Negro. He said he wished to adopt her offspring as atonement for his guilt in murdering the Jews.

'Very soon, there were a number of these children who had reached the age where they could be taken on as apprentices in various trades. So many job offerings were made to them that it aroused suspicions, which, as it turned out, were not unjustified. These little chocolate-coloured boys, many employers thought, were sure to be an attraction as lift operators, counter boys in pastry shops, models for advertising billboards, and doormen in front of fashion salons. Germany's career-guidance office has put a stop to that little game.'

What did the parents of our library visitors look like? What occupied their thoughts and their time? What kind of home life did these children who came to us have? We sent out invitations for a tea party (the English are not the only ones who know the magic of this drink).

[120]

The parents came in throngs. We had to seat some of them on small chairs made for children. Trying to guess which parents belonged to which children became an exciting party game. Perhaps many of our little angels in the library were devils at home, or vice versa. And their clothing didn't give much away. At most, big patches said something for the mother's industry.

There they sat over their cups of tea, looking about curiously – provincial judges from the high court, pastry cooks, bus conductors, career women, consuls, housewives, pediatricians, university professors, converted and hard-line Nazis, conservatives, socialists, Catholics, Protestants, Germans, Americans, Swiss, French. What a fascinating mixture they were.

As might have been expected, we talked to our guests about an extremely exciting subject – their children. They knew no more or less about them than any other generation of parents, yet their relation to their children was a much more complicated one. There were vast stretches of wilderness in the parents' lives over which they had spread a blanket of silence and embarrassment. How often does anyone himself have any clear idea or understanding of experiences that have scarcely been endured?

To those in our organization, who did not have to strive after such truths but had made the attainment of them one of their main goals, witnessing this gap between generations was painful. Many of the parents hung between tears and laughter as they sat staring at us and nibbling their biscuits.

The high point of the evening was a reading from various children's books, given by some aspiring young actors. This was their first stage, and they performed. Afterwards there was stormy applause and the decision was made on the spot to form a parents' council which would appoint a representative to the library board. Parents' night subsequently became a permanent feature. Librarians in other parts of Germany shook their heads. They had never heard of such a thing.

Serious-minded pedagogues can't hold a candle to puppets when it comes to competition between the two. Children love puppets, that's the secret. We hired artists to make ours to order – artists like Fritz Eichler and Franz Schadt, who specialized in puppets. What an audience we had for our *première* of 'The King Who Couldn't Laugh,' and for 'Once One Times One Equals One,' the story of three feuding villagers who found happiness and prosperity only after they had made peace with each other. Every performance was like a *première*, because there always were new variations. The puppets did nicely on their own, directing lusty gibes at their audience, whose number had to be curtailed because of fire precautions. The puppet theatre gained international fame, though a world tour that had been offered foundered on the rocks of international bureaucracy.

Regarding films, we couldn't commission the production of our own, but there were many others available. There were films about the wide, wide world, about peoples of foreign lands, about famous persons, as well as regular feature films and fairy tales adapted for the screen. What a treat they were for people then, when there were no cinemas on every street corner as there are now. One memorable showing was of Schweizer's film *Marie Luise*. The children identified with her deeply. The book was on our shelves, but now they were seeing Marie Luise with their own eyes. Our free films were always attended by capacity audiences.

One of the most controversial issues of the library was the artist's studio for the children. Ferdinand Steidle, a gifted painter and art teacher, reigned like an idiosyncratic monarch in the enlarged attic of our building. And woe be to anybody subject to his sceptre when he didn't wish to be disturbed.

The children arrived in cheerful throngs, with three-, four- and five-year-olds among them. Drawing paper itself was much too costly to pass round, but there was always plenty of brown wrapping paper and newsprint, and people donated brushes and water colours for the children to work with. They romped about on the wide expanse of surface as though they were playing on a frozen lake, and gave no heed to the confining shores.

The maestro would tell a fairy tale, a biblical story, or a story out of a child's everyday experience. The children would raise objections, ask questions, or even reject the subject completely and demand another one. The area was wide, the results often amazing. They painted Adam and Eve, the Christ child in the manger, and marvellous things like flying carpets, little Nils Holgersson's wild goose, the Trojan horse, Jonah's whale and, of course, the Flood and Noah's Ark. When the surprised teacher would discover a strange, shaggy creature tugging at Noah's coat and carefully inquired about it, he was told *'Mais c'est Asso, mon chien!'* (But that's Asso, my dog). These children bridged the limits of time and space in bold leaps. Other subjects they painted were 'Flower Seller,' 'The Ice Cream Woman,' 'Family Outing,' 'Robinson Crusoe,' 'Market Day,' and 'The Fair.'

One of the great adventures was a project to make a wall-hanging, which became not a wall-hanging at all but a giant mural representing the children's communal effort. Various subjects to be painted were assigned around the general theme 'Circus.' One child specialized in horses, another in apes and lions, one was an expert on clowns and one on ice cream sellers. The smaller girls were especially keen on portraying tightrope walkers and dancers leaping through hoops.

I christened these communal pictures, 'Paint Brush Conversations.' In the play of painting the children learned how to work co-operatively, picking up where another child had left off so that the integrity of the whole remained undisturbed. And experiences such as these were doubly valuable where the children were of different nationalities. How I would have liked to place the leaders of the great powers side by side in front of an enormous white canvas and have them paint their picture of a united world.

A quite special mural was painted in 1953 with the object of presenting it to Prince Charles and Princess Anne, on the occasion of the coronation of the Queen of England. It portrayed upper

Bavaria with its mountains and lakes, farmhouses with geraniums in window boxes, baroque churches and monasteries, peasants in their traditional dresses, and finally a beer wagon with its usual team of four white horses. It was so evocative and real you wanted to walk right into the picture.

Unfortunately the English royal couple could not simply walk in and make it theirs, because a strict protocol ruled against gifts. The wonderful present was returned promptly with a letter from the queen's secretary saying that the royal family regretted that they could not accept such a gift.

I didn't dare reveal this crushing rejection to the children, for how could they have understood such a thing? Instead, I phoned the foreign ministry in Bonn and begged them to intervene diplomatically in our behalf. They obliged, and the picture was sent back to London, this time to the German Embassy. An envoy, extremely optimistic it seemed, personally carried it under his arm and succeeded in accomplishing his difficult mission. A short time later a letter of thanks arrived for us, bearing the queen's coat of arms. The children triumphantly hung the letter on the wall.

Can a child actually see himself? Does he have any idea of his own unique little ego? Is he aware of anything beyond the freckles on his nose? We undertook the original and fascinating project of assembling children's self-portraits from all over the world. The first request was sent out in the autumn of 1950. During the next year and a half four thousand self-portraits descended on us from thirty nations, forming a unique collection of inexhaustible variety.

'. . . to the mind of a child, the self is a remote and exotic topic because when left to themselves, children's interest and attention always is directed away and outside of their own beings . . .' wrote Professor Emil Preetorius, the chairman of our jury. 'Turning towards his self, towards his singular personality, his singular face, means a total readjustment of the child's spirit and a shift of viewpoint not achieved without a certain danger to his innocent mind . . . It is as surprising as it is significant that this apparent danger to children of almost all races can only occasionally be detected. This is because the child-artist is still – in Dürer's beautiful words – 'inwardly full of images'. These paintings *par coeur* are the essence of childhood.

'Observing this wealth of children's paintings, one is struck by two things: all these renderings bear a common stamp transcending national boundaries, and the "It" has not yet become an "I", with all its consequent limitations. In spite of these similarities, though, closer observation reveals the fine distinctions resulting from individual cultures and the special features of locale and blood, belief and history, of those cultures . . .'

Time and again we jury members were fascinated by the children's honesty, which sometimes actually approached the grotesque, and their devil-may-care air of courage. If a child's ears stuck out slightly in real life, he would paint them as protruding at right angles; a few summer freckles were turned into a whole network of freckles, and noses à la Pinocchio were represented by the dozens. One of our library children painted a full-length portrait of herself with a shadow around the region of the stomach that was difficult to identify immediately. She later explained, 'That's a fish. I had a fish for dinner, you know.'

The exhibition of self-portraits, called '*Ich Selbst – Myself – Moi Même,*' travelled around the world. Columbia University in New York City even requested a second showing, 'for purposes of study'. Walking through the exhibition rooms I saw a 'Children's United Nations' looking out at us hopefully.

'Wedding' was the subject of another exhibition of paintings which drew 5,844 entries from twenty-eight nations. Here the children were given the opportunity to portray the dress, manners, and customs of their country. And what a panorama it was! The love of story-telling was evident everywhere you turned; though, unfortunately, so was a tendency to copy. The splendours of fairy tales were reflected in paint, and daydreams were given visible form. The conventional and original stood side by side, and unconscious humour was pictured in great detail: bridegrooms in flower-decked coaches cowering in fear before their garlanded brides, who almost vanished in the rich upholstery. In a painting from England a bride was reversing custom and carrying her new bridegroom over the threshold of their new home. Another couple were in the middle of their marriage vows in an airplane, while a black storm cloud gathered above and below them, boding no good . . .

Even so, our artist's studio was a bone of contention and remains so today. Bonn in particular saw it as a fit object to attack; apparently it had become a ministerial headache. Perhaps we were asking them to stretch their imaginations too far. What did children's paintings have to do with libraries? Civil servants had by no means caught up with the modern conception of such an institution and they kept sending us injunctions in the sterile jargon of officialdom: the studio was not to be included in the budget statements. To this date this rather high-handed order has never been complied with, thanks to the faithful support of our 'connections', and I pray that it will remain that way through the future. Children's books and children's art belong together.

A Children's United Nations – it was not the self-portraits alone that kept conjuring up this idea in my head. I saw it even in my dreams. But to realize such a dream, you almost always have to go after it yourself. And that is what I did.

One day the children were handed a special leaflet.

'You must have heard of the United Nations – the U.N. – where delegates from sixty different countries work together to establish international understanding and world peace.

'We would like to conduct an experimental Children's United Nations here at IYL. I am afraid that we will not be able to bring children from sixty countries to Munich by air, so we are asking you to act as delegates from the sixty countries yourselves. Choose that country which you find of especial interest and importance.

There are to be two delegates from each of those countries. The age of air travel has brought people closer together physically, and it is very necessary for them to get to know and understand one another, too.

'Every month there will be a General Assembly where discussions will be held on subjects you select yourselves. The IYL will furnish you with books, newspapers, photographs, maps, and gramophone records. We are inviting boys and girls between the ages of 12 to 16 years old, who are interested, to register with the IYL, where you can obtain further information.

U.N. members as of September 28, 1950:

Abyssinia, Afghanistan, Argentina, Australia, Belgium, Bolivia, Brazil, Burma, Canada, Chile, China, Colombia, Costa Rica, Cuba, Czechoslovakia, Denmark, Dominican Republic, Ecuador, El Salvador, England, France, Greece, Guatemala, Haiti, Honduras, Iceland, India, Indonesia, Iran, Iraq, Israel, Lebanon, Liberia, Luxembourg, Netherlands, New Zealand, Nicaragua, Norway, Pakistan, Panama, Paraguay, Peru, Philippines, Poland, Saudi Arabia, South Africa, Sweden, Syria, Thailand, Turkey, Ukraine, Uruguay, U.S.A., USSR, Venezuela, White Russia, Yemen, Yugoslavia.

'The youth after the war threw all ideals overboard' – what a ridiculous generalization that was. *These* young people, at any rate, provided constant proof of the contrary. They formed long lines in front of the announcement I had tacked up, and the very popularity of the Children's U.N. gave promise of a new world.

We did get into trouble at the beginning over choosing delegates. We had limited the number allocated to each country to two, but no one had foreseen the fierce competition that would result. The U.S.A., whose appeal was tremendous, led the list. Then came England, Sweden, Iceland, and the Netherlands. The distant lands like India, Brazil, Chile, Thailand, and Haiti were attractive, too. Germany was only an observer nation at the real U.N., but she achieved delegate status in ours. A rather shy fifth-grader entered his name as delegate for Russia – 'Russia, not the Soviet Union,' he insisted. And two Transylvania girls put in their bids for Czechoslovakia.

At once these children went out in droves to cram up on knowledge about 'their' countries. They visited consulates, travel agencies, airline offices, museums and libraries. I tapped the library's clay piggy bank, and it sounded hollow. Where were we going to get the money for all the new books we would need?

An ideal forum-place for our U.N. was the art studio. The official inauguration of the Children's U.N. took place on January 16, 1954. The delegates, bursting with pride, sat down at the tables at places decorated with the flags of their countries, all scrubbed and combed, and all adopting a diplomatic decorum. Their big brothers in New York weren't going to outclass them. And no one was going to muzzle these children, either, because there wasn't a topic that could intimidate them, no matter how delicate or difficult. On one occasion, discussing various forms of government, they rejected dictatorship in any shape or form and advanced the idea of freedom as the highest goal of all.

It was only fitting then that at one of the first sessions the motion was made to change the name of their organization from 'Children's U.N.' to 'Young People's U.N.' 'We're not children any more,' they insisted. An effort to present childhood as a desirable state was shot to the ground. 'We had to take part in the war when we were only six,' they said, 'and afterwards we weren't allowed to be children, though we would have liked to be that then.'

A flood of effective argumentation followed.

'I tramped from Dresden to Nürnberg with only my two little sisters, and I was so intent on getting away that I forgot my sixth birthday.'

'I was jailed in my village just for stealing a loaf of bread.'

'When bomb splinters hit my mother, I had to make an emergency dressing for her with my handkerchief, or otherwise she would have bled to death. I was seven then.'

These words brought a saying of Jean Paul's to my mind:

'Wipe away the tears of children, rain is so damaging to buds.'

What other topics did the children, who were now young people, discuss?

'Must we have to keep an army for world peace?' They agreed on a United Nations Peace Force.

'Is racial segregation warranted?' The vote was a flat no, with the United States in particular coming in for some harsh words. *Uncle Tom's Cabin* wasn't the only source of information the delegates had.

'Do we need an international language?' A lively spokesman for Esperanto took the floor and crowned her plea with an example of this attempt at a universal language. It didn't go over very well.

'It's a patchwork of stolen languages,' they cried scornfully. 'And it's much harder to learn than a real language.'

'Why make up an artificial world language when the whole world speaks English anyway?'

'French always has been the language of diplomacy,' the French delegate offered, but he was outnumbered.

One boy even brought up Latin. 'Latin is the language of the church,' he said, but he, too, was defeated. The delegates probably were thinking of their homework

At the close of the debate, a young sceptic climbed to his feet and gave his views on the subject. 'Why work yourselves up?' he said. 'The universal language some day might be Chinese. Who can tell?'

'Should young people concern themselves with politics?' Plainly, the discussion that followed showed that they considered such involvement as their somewhat bitter duty. The very idea of the Young People's U.N. in itself was an answer to that question. The essence of their debate was: 'Politics, yes, party politics, no.'

'Our stand on the Children's Charter.' This debate highlighted the importance of the Young People's U.N. in its deepest sense, which no longer could be considered as mere child's play. Even the doubting Thomases were convinced. The real United Nations had recently drafted a 'Children's Charter' to ensure the 'normal and healthy development of every child in freedom and dignity.' Even now it was being submitted to the Human Rights section for ratification. It might still be possible to make suggestions.

The Charter as it was drafted was read aloud at the opening of the session. The children, completely hushed, listened in silence. The grave, interested faces of the children were unforgettable. At the reading of the paragraph which maintained that children should no longer be helpless at the hands of their elders, the whole assembly broke out in applause.

One delegate shouted, 'Adults don't always, I'm afraid, have the care and protection of children at heart.'

'Children often have to show patience with grown-ups, too,' one girl said.

'And don't forget the plight of the latchkey children,' several voices broke in. 'Our mothers would much rather stay at home than have to hang the key around our necks.'

Not only were these children critical, their understanding of these complicated relationships was far beyond their years.

One of the main concerns of the actual Children's Charter was with orphans. After this section was read, a swarm of hands shot up in protest.

'Why not children from broken homes, too?' they wanted to know.

Broken homes? Suddenly I saw the writing on the wall.

'Are there many children from broken homes here?' I asked.

One third of the children raised their hands, conclusively demonstrating that something must be done. We then passed a resolution: The Young People's U.N. asks the real U.N. to include children from broken homes in the Charter.

Another gap was next discovered: Children must never be forced to bear arms.

This precipitated one story after another of their experiences in the Hitler Youth and the Werewolf.

[130]

'Nothing like that can ever happen again!'

'It is happening again,' a girl cried out. 'It's happening in Korea every day.' She was a Korean war refugee and should have known.

The minutes of the session, including the two proposals, were mailed special delivery to the Commission on Human Rights in New York. I am grieved to report that the U.N. never sent its little brother organization a reply.

By way of compensation, however, Luther Evans, then director-general of UNESCO, made a goodwill visit to one session of the Young People's U.N., accompanied by some other U.N. delegates. The International Youth Library in the meantime had been designated an Associated Project of UNESCO. The delegates from India and their child counterparts shook hands enthusiastically.

The world-wide epidemic of conference-itis also infected the IYL. We boldly proposed a conference of special librarians who were employed by large companies. Leading industrial concerns in Germany had risen again like the Phoenix, and the effects of their expansion already could be felt. Before the war, every company had its own library. Here was a unique opportunity to spread the idea of international understanding through children's books to a wider sector of the population. People from personnel offices, librarians, company welfare workers, editors of industrial magazines, career counsellors, all made their way through the January snows of 1954 to the building on Kaulbachstrasse. Representatives from chemical plants and from the motor and photographic industry came and studied our model for an IYL of industry.

Speaking with the tongues of angels, we gave a running commentary and showed photographs of factory workers happily bringing home books for their children in the evening, books to read aloud within the family circle, instead of seeking diversion in the tavern next door. Secretly, of course, we were hoping for bigger gains. If such a thing as re-education did exist at all, this provided a unique opportunity to accomplish it.

To our astonishment, one representative after another stood up and lamented the emptiness of their cash box. Considering the new construction and reconstruction, they had not yet arrived at the point where they could consider the cultural side of things. We said we were sorry and advised the poor souls not to be deterred.

The audience, nodded, their pencils racing across the page; everything we said was taken down in shorthand. A programme was put together finally which we had no reason to be ashamed of. And, miracle of miracles, it even got beyond the paper it was written on. Some of its features were:

1. The establishment of a children's book section in company libraries as a token gesture towards promoting international understanding.

2. The shipment of crates of books, to be known as 'Treasure Chests,' through the IYL.

3. Training of company librarians.

4. Distribution of booklists.

5. Tours of our model library.

We were bombarded with invitations to the openings of company libraries, and several large firms enlarged their libraries so as to incorporate children's painting displays. Blue and white collar workers both showed enormous interest, and publishers and booksellers won a new market for children's books. Maria Wolff, the highly talented daughter of the publisher Kurt Wolff, became a special envoy in this field.

If only for the record, it must be noted that the International Youth Library had to content itself as usual with intangible rewards, although it would by no means have rejected material ones. It was sobering to realize that German industry would have to be appealed to, enabling us to open a separate account for those undertakings which the Rockefeller Foundation grant did not cover and towards which the federal audit office showed little sympathy. To be sure, the federal audit office was only an earth-bound authority, but among other ministries and by officialdom in general it was regarded with positive reverence. We were what is known as a semi-governmental institution, and several ministries held our purse strings and had us on other strings as well. This purse string was at the same time a lifeline and a noose. For myself, I liked freedom, but when it came to charity I preferred the private kind over the public any time.

Although it cost a great struggle to do it, I sat down and composed a letter to Alfred Krupp von Bohlen u. Halbach, asking him if he would act as the German counterpart to the Rockefeller Foundation. Children's books instead of cannon – it was an attractive slogan.

A rather belated reply came from the Villa Hügel. Herr von Bohlen u. Halbach was away, cruising through southern waters on his yacht. My request would have to wait. Weeks later another letter arrived signed by a secretary. There should have been a black border around it, but there wasn't. Herr Krupp von Bohlen u. Halbach sent his regrets, the lettter stated, but all his charitable donations were made to the Associated Foundation of German Industries, to whom our application had been passed on. For burial, the letter might have added.

For we already knew about this foundation, having often made pilgrimages to its Rhine location, returning with nothing to show for our trip but fine-sounding phrases. Unlike the Impressionists and Expressionists, children's books cannot be hung in executive offices. Nor can they be placed on marble pedestals like pieces of sculpture. And even worse, they are duds when it comes to a political battle, and will never win anybody a seat in a provincial or federal legislature. So, whether we wanted to or not, we had to accept the fact that our irresistable ambassadors had been shown to the door.

Of great comfort to us were the directors of the humanities division of the Rockefeller Foundation, who one by one came to visit us. Every one of them was as tall as a tree in the forest.

None would let you address them by their titles, and they were all humanists in the truest sense of the word.

Edward D'Arms, who long ago had taken the IYL under his personal wing, deserved the order of merit medal whether we had one to bestow or not.

What a fine group of people came through our house on Kaulbachstrasse in those days! Ellen McCloy, wife of the American military governor, wrote enthusiastically:

> Haus im Walde
> Bad Homburg
> 25 January 1950

Dear Mrs Lepman:

I will always remember the delightful afternoon I spent in your extraordinary library. Not only is it lovely and cosy, but it radiates so much hope and warm feeling. I am very grateful to you for having invited me. I do hope Mr McCloy will be able to share this experience with me some day soon.

At this moment there are so many good and bad things in the world around us. Your library is one of the truly good things, and it has been an inspiration to have had a share in it even for a short while.

Hoping that we meet again soon,

> Very sincerely,
> Ellen McCloy.

Bright and charming Ellen McCloy! She spoke German fluently and was always drowned in requests from German women asking her for help. She sat at her desk night after night examining each individual case. Mr McCloy, who came hobbling into the library one day with a plaster cast on his leg, smiled proudly at his wife's great popularity.

Mr McCloy's German partner, Federal President Theodor Heuss, paid his first visit to the library under particularly amusing circumstances. His schedule in Munich was often so overcrowded that he didn't have a minute to spare for personal invitations. We wondered if he could circumvent protocol with a little trick. While his official car from the state chancellory waited for him outside the main gate of the *Vier Jahreszeiten* hotel, Mr Heuss and his private secretary Dr Bott slipped through a side door, signalled for the nearest taxi, and drove straight to the IYL. Jubilant as a schoolboy who had outwitted his mentor, he walked through the rooms delighting everybody with his knowledge of books, and he would have liked nothing better than to have picked up a brush and begun painting on one of the children's easels. Then he climbed back into his taxi as the gentlemen from the government continued their frantic search for him.

Martin Buber came to visit us once on a trip from Israel. I personally welcomed him at the door, out of respect for such an eminent guest. He looked the way a child imagines God to be, or the prophet Elijah in his chariot of fire. He regarded the books with a kind smile, asking questions that showed his vast knowledge, and as he walked he tossed out words of wisdom like flowers to those around him.

'Look at this man,' I wanted to shout out loud. 'It was only by a miracle that he escaped Hitler's madness.' Then I happened to look at the faces of people standing around us. They stared at the floor and one young librarian was crying. Perhaps one should not speak of such things, but they are a part of the mosaic of experience.

On the fifth anniversary of the IYL, our little trainee librarian announced that a Mr Wilder was here. 'A nice gentleman with flowers,' she said. Who could that be? I wondered. But when he appeared I knew him at once as Thornton Wilder. In his hand he was carrying a bouquet that radiated all the colours of autumn. He embraced me and said, 'This is for your beautiful idea, and the way you've made it work.' That morning he had read a notice in the newspaper about our anniversary and he had impulsively set out to pay us a visit.

Assistants came to work with us from all corners of the compass, for here at the IYL there was a unique educational facility they had never worked with before. UNESCO sent us Shakuntala Bhatawdekar from the famous New Delhi library.

Shakuntala, whose name sounded like music, was given the job of compiling a catalogue of international children's books for use in Asiatic countries, and the IYL was the ideal place for her research. She steadfastly refused to include in her list Jean de Brunhoff's *Babar* because, she said, 'The children of India will never believe in a talking elephant. Elephants are not something in a zoo to them, as they are to your children.' Singing American cows were rejected just as stubbornly. 'Cows are sacred animals in India,' she said. 'And besides that, they do not sing.' Shakuntala, who wore a different and magnificent sari every day, was as charming as she was bright.

It was at this time that I began to sense the difficulties in working co-operatively with the developing countries, and I tried to learn all I could about the Asiatic attitude towards children's books. I don't pretend that I ever succeeded.

Momoko Ishii from Tokyo was the next guest to visit the IYL, and she remained with us for several months. Though she wore western clothing, she padded through the rooms with all the grace of Japanese women. Only a short time before her country had honoured her with a children's book award for *Nobi in the Clouds*, and it was about to be brought out by a German children's book publisher. With comical despair she told us how she had been trying to convey the magical quality of Japanese cherry blossoms to the illustrator assigned to the book, who could not catch the faintest idea of what she meant. Finally the difference in their two worlds struck her, and to express it she shouted at him, 'Japanese children *don't* dance the Bavarian *Schuhplattler!*' Pronouncing the word almost broke her tongue.

'Co-ordination: Harmonious adjustment or functioning,' so reads the dictionary definition. This was precisely what was lacking in the field of children's books in the period immediately after the war. It occurred to us that we might provide a common platform for all those interested in children's books, by holding a conference for such people as writers, illustrators, publishers, booksellers, librarians, educators, art teachers, psychiatrists, not to mention representatives from the new mass media industry of films, radio and television.

From a private list I had made up of Who's Who in children's literature, sixty invitations were cast to the winds like trial balloons in the autumn of 1951, with no weather forecast on which one could rely.

In a few days the first telegrams and cables of acceptance began blowing in, and along with them urgent requests from people who had not been invited and wished to be included. I reasoned that the moment had come to find a chairman for the conference. How we got one is an amusing story.

Ortega y Gasset at the time was a guest lecturer at the University of Munich. I immediately thought of getting him to set an intellectual tone for the conference. I held no illusions about the presumptuousness of my plan. In spite of that, I sat down at my desk and wrote a letter to the famous philosopher. I carried the letter to the post box myself.

Precious days flew by, and nothing happened. I began secretly to tremble. But evidently I hadn't lost my appetite, for each day I went to my favourite little restaurant round the corner which was called the Halali.

One day I entered the place and sat down at the only empty table. All about me diners were devouring giant portions of liver dumplings and smoked pork with sauerkraut. It was a pleasure – albeit not exactly an aesthetic one – to watch them gorge themselves. Hunger finally had been banished from postwar Germany.

Anyway, pretty soon a man walked up to my table and politely asked if he might sit with me, since the other tables were taken. I invited him to sit down. While he was studying the menu I stole frequent glances at him. His face seemed vaguely familiar, and it was a face not easily forgotten. I leafed hurried through my memory and all at once it came to me – this was Professor Ortega y Gasset. That guardian angel of mine had been working overtime and had led him to my table.

That is exactly what I said to him as I started a conversation, my heart beating a mile a minute. At first he looked at me in dismay, then amusement.

'Oh, you're the one who wrote to me,' he said. 'I was just on the point of sending you a note, declining your invitation. I deeply regret it, of course, but I never take on duties beyond my commitment to the university.'

'Yes, but even renowned professors of philosophy must obey the angels,' I replied. 'How can you defy so obvious a manifestation of heavenly will?'

And with that I had won him.

Meanwhile, telegrams and cables were coming and going in a torrent. The number of participants increased from sixty to two hundred and fifty. Since our rooms in the library could not be expanded, the conference was transferred to the *Prinz Carl Palais*, where at least we could feel at home.

There, before a glittering international audience, Ortega y Gasset made his memorable speech, in impeccable German with an equally impeccable Spanish accent. It was entitled, 'The educational paradox, and the idea of a myth-building education.'

'Educators who really wish to be in tune with the times,' he said, 'must realize how much our horizons have been expanded in the last few decades . . . A temporary acceleration of political activity in Europe now is being followed by an exemplary depreciation of all things political. Soon they will disappear from the forefront of human concerns, and it will become clear that education no longer will have to adapt itself to politics, but that politics will have to adapt itself to education. Which is what Plato dreamed of long ago . . .

'The educator may suggest giving priority in school to newspapers over literature. But the newspaper is no expression of the spirit of life. All it is, purely and simply, is an expression of life's superficialities and its changing aspects day to day. The deeper, more personal and significant aspects of life are almost entirely excluded . . . The problem of education always has been one of limitations.'

After these preliminary remarks, he continued.

'We must distinguish between three important species of vital functions. First, the use of tools and machines; second, the function of the organs that spontaneously generate life; third, that elemental vital spark that animates us all – feelings and emotions, courage and curiosity, love and hate, the hope to enjoy and prevail, confidence in oneself and in the world, memory, the capacity for wonder and worship. Education, then, is the training of this inner being in the child . . .

'The child should be raised in an atmosphere of bold, generous, ambitious, and enthusiastic emotions. Mythical figures such as Hercules and Ulysses will for ever be perfect ones for the child because, like all mythology, they generate a spirit of inexhaustible enthusiasm.'

However, Ortega y Gasset found *Don Quixote* far too modern in spirit to be included as a book for school children. '. . . enormously complicated, radical, ironic, not a book for children,' he said.

'We adults are grounded in a world we look upon as a definitive point of reference,' he went on. 'The child can only move with uncertainty in the setting our souls inhabit. Pedagogy has always tried to clip the wings of childhood. The adult world obstructs childhood, suppresses it, maims it, and distorts its spirit . . . But maturity and culture are not the creations of the adult and the sage, but of the child and the savage within us. Let us raise our children, as children forgetting as completely as we can that they will be adults some day. The best human being is never the man who has been least a child, but the man who still preserves the rich treasure of childhood in his heart. As Plato said long before us, we must never let the child within us die.

'The twentieth century surpasses the nineteenth in proportion as it negates the peculiarities of the former century. Such a negation, however, presumes that the past century lives on in the present. Maturity is not a dissolving away from childhood, but a bringing together of childhood . . . The songs of poets, the words of the wise, the genius of politicians are no more than grown-up echoes of the voices that have been long held in check and that wish to flourish as the eternal child.'

The rousing and impassioned words of Ortega y Gasset's *Cantus firmus* hung like a living presence over the rest of the conference.

The next thrill for the participants, though of course of a different nature, was a speech delivered from the platform on 'Cruelty in Fairy Tales', Lisa Tetzner defined cruelty as the negative principle to be found in the heart of every human being and thus not something that could be erased by denying its existence. She called for recognition of the fact that selection of fairy tales, considered in relation to the singular psychological needs of postwar children, demanded great psychological insight.

During the next few days all aspects of literature for children and young people were discussed by prominent people from many nations. Among them were Richard Bamberger, Vienna; Fritz Brunner, Zürich; Miss W. E. S. Coops, UNESCO in Paris; Anton Fingerle, Munich; Erich Kästner, Munich; Kurt Kläber, Carona; Heinrich Lades, Bonn; Emil Oprecht, Zürich; Hanns Ott, Bonn; Luise Rinser, Munich; Hans Rabén, Stockholm; and Hans Sauerländer, Aarau. Naturally, there also was a delegation from the Youth Committee of the IYL, the very young people who were being discussed, who were given an opportunity to speak for themselves.

This conference was one of the first international cultural affairs to be held on German soil following the war, and the air was filled with tension. Describing a strange and distorted history of past events, one German educator tried to represent the wartime suffering of his country's children as being by far the most tragic

[140]

of all. A woman from Holland jumped to her feet and in tearful protest cried out, 'Rotterdam!' Far too many in Germany were living in the dangerous delusion that they could rid themselves of their Nazi past with a shrug. In the midst of the festive hall, a sense of sadness stole over me. And yet, in spite of the differences among us, the possibilities of co-operative effort could be seen, too: in spreading around the best in children's literature, in setting standards against bad books, in the exchange of classic and contemporary children's books, in the publication of book lists and discussion of current problems in children's literature. But the most essential point was the fostering of tolerance and international understanding.

On a bleak, wintry Sunday, the 18th November, 1951, the establishment of the International Board on Books for Young People was unanimously approved.

The child was born. Now it had to prove its viability.

Zürich and Switzerland were selected as the home and permanent seat of the international board. True world-awareness has always been at home in Switzerland.

Zürich's famous Federal Institute of Technology placed one of its lecture halls at our disposal for our first general meeting. Two hundred participants trooped in to discuss 'Current Affairs and Children's Literature.' Otto Binder, secretary-general of our model, Pro Juventute, presided as our first president, and he demonstrated that the Swiss are also distinguished for their sense of humour.

A stormy debate got under way on comic books, which in the opinion of many should be wiped off the face of the earth, certainly a most ambitious proposal. The conservatives were for encouraging good comic strips, and were not prepared to damn altogether the principle of telling stories by pictures. This quarrel continues even today. It is an issue with many gradients between the black and white.

[141]

A pleasant interlude was provided when Switzerland's two great illustrators – Hans Fischer and Alois Carigiet – picked up pieces of chalk and sketched some ingenious pictures on the Federal Institute's blackboards, which normally were devoted to mathematical formulae. The symbol for F sharp became a splendid specimen of a rooster that everybody expected to start crowing any minute.

Why should only adult books be considered for the Nobel Prize? It was high time for it to have a little brother, so ran the thinking that brought about the Hans Christian Andersen Prize. The gilded medal engraved with the head of the Danish storyteller is awarded by an international jury to a contemporary author for an outstanding book, or, as is the practice today, for the whole body of his work. The award was promptly christened 'The little Nobel Prize,' and in many ways it deserved this title. Unfortunately though, not in every way, for no cheque for a staggering amount of money is pressed into the winner's hand; he must be content with the honour. However, this is enormous, and on the basis of it he can hope to have his work translated into many languages. To date the award has been received by Eleanor Farjeon of England, Astrid Lindgren of Sweden, Erich Kästner of Germany, Meindert De Jong of the United States, René Guillot of France, Tove Jansson of Finland, and by the founder of the International Youth Library and the International Board on Books for Young People, Jella Lepman.

The Honours List and list of runners-up for the Hans Christian Andersen Prize acquaints the world with the best children's books of all nations. The biennial Congress of the International Board on Books for Young People, which has been held in Vienna, Stockholm, Florence, Luxembourg, Hamburg and Madrid, has shown the world that far from being the stepchild of great literature, children's books are well on their way to taking a place in the front ranks.

[142]

Germany now was called a 'wonderland', for the transformation was breathtaking, even uncanny. The children could place a dozen books under their pillows, and all in de luxe editions. Much had changed since the dark days in Berlin of 1946.

'How do you feel in the role of Alice in Wonderland?' an English visitor asked with obvious irony. If I were to look at the situation objectively, in many ways I would have preferred those first years after the war with the dimly lit streets, the fourteen-hour work days, and the pioneering spirit that went with it, to the neon lighting, the eight-hour day, and bureaucracy and fellow-travelling that in the present spread their poisons like an epidemic. Of course I was glad to see the children with plump faces instead of hollow cheeks, but still there had been something intangible, perhaps the spirit of the times. Though then it had often seemed to me to be more of a ghost than a spirit.

I attended the meetings that were to decide the future development of the IYL, with children's books in one hand and a sword in the other. Sensible, well-meaning men sat around the circular Biedermeier table in the house on Kaulbachstrasse, most of those men in important official posts with the government. A ministry in Bonn now was the chief source of our funds, and on that fact it claimed the right to guide our policy. Bonn's conception of our mission and our own original conception of an International Youth Library came to be more and more at odds, both openly and covertly. Nothing could sway me from my view of international understanding through children's books, from our free, creative library, with all of its activities – a word that, significantly, does not translate into German. Unfortunately our critics in Bonn held a much more limited view, one which was more of an information centre for German publishers and educators. Foreign books, perhaps – but what was the point of inviting children to such a library? Why have book discussion groups, foreign language classes, a Young People's U.N.? And why – crowning folly – an art studio! From the very beginning children came before index cards – that, obviously, was symptomatic of our whole outlook.

I probably had never fully realized how hard it must have been for the authorities to make room in their ministerial household for such a strange bird as ours. If you were lucky enough to deal with enlightened state secretaries and ministers, there were always side doors that could be entered – but why go in by side doors? Wasn't Germany being given, in this organization, a tremendous opportunity to sponsor an international achievement of distinction?

One particularly bitter battle arose over a bookmobile, a library on wheels. We had frequently told our friends in America how wonderful such a vehicle would be for exhibiting a modern international library and its methods in the major cities of Germany and other countries.

An anonymous benefactress from far-away Texas had given in to the blandishments of the A.L.A. on our behalf, and we were informed in exuberant terms that a cheque was on its way.

I could hardly wait for the next meeting to announce this happy news. But the proposal met with a general shaking of heads. What new complications would this bookmobile bring? The purchase of books, petrol, salary for another librarian. An air of depression settled over the meeting, while I held back tears of disappointment. My bookmobile was something straight out of a fairy tale, and here it was being stripped of all its glory. They were, in fact, considering the return of the gift. All that prevented them from doing so, they decided, were reasons of diplomacy!

Not every story has a happy ending. The bookmobile, a marvellous example of its kind, was delivered in the autumn of 1956. It made its maiden trip in the driving rain of the Bavarian forest. This critically book-starved area was not far from us, so not much petrol was needed. With all respect to the people in this underdeveloped strip in Germany's land of miracles, what they really needed was a well-organized German public library service. The

Bavarian forest was like Potemkin's village as far as the rest of the world was concerned.

After its service in this region, the bookmobile was sent to hibernate in a corrugated tin hut. It might still be there had not UNESCO awakened it with a princely kiss and sent it into service in another land.

vii

Politics is a far-reaching concept that manages to touch upon every area of our lives. Two world wars in this century have given people a shattering object lesson. Even those nations which formerly were nearly untouched by civilization could not persist in isolation any longer. A new idea stirred the minds of men – aid to the developing countries.

One day in the spring of 1956 I was sitting in my room, where so many plans had been conceived and set in motion. Across from me sat Mr D'Arms of the Rockefeller Foundation, who was telling me about a world project for developing countries which would include the Rockefeller, Ford, and Middle East Foundations, as well as UNESCO. Suddenly he looked at me and said, 'Would you like children's books to be part of the programme?'

This was no rhetorical question, I felt sure. This would be a unique opportunity to spread the idea of international understanding through children's books to countries that were just coming into their own. Once more, fate was knocking at my door. I accepted the offer and the arrangements were made.

The first leg of my journey was to the United States. Where 'Mission for Children' was what my first trip to America could have been called, this one could be entitled, 'A Thanksgiving Journey for Children.'

Sitting at my hotel room window soon after arriving, surrounded by the fragrance of flowers sent me by well-wishers, the old magic of Manhattan swept through me anew. On that first trip here I had travelled through the United States with a new idea for bringing nations together, and that bold dream had come true. But the United States still was without peer as the land of children's books, and almost at once the wild activities began. I was swept up by the tide of Children's Book Week; together with Eleanor Roosevelt and Anne Carroll Moore, a moving force behind America's libraries for children, I was a guest speaker at the fiftieth anniversary celebration for the New York Public Library.

Frederic Melcher, president of the American Publishers Association, gave a party in my honour at the Roosevelt Hotel. This guiding spirit of children's books himself led me into the reception hall. In spite of the fact that I had memorized the speech I had planned to give, before such an imposing audience I couldn't find a word to say.

My first contact with the developing countries had been made with our library children during Story Hour. Only later did I realize that we had a new version of *Gulliver's Travels* on our hands. Here, now, was a 'Gulliver' coming from an overdeveloped nation to visit an underdeveloped one, and after arriving home after a series of adventures he would find that he himself was now numbered among the underdeveloped. It was an alarming thought. For the first time I clearly saw just what humanity was embarking upon with its mania for development, and it was too late to send out warnings. The East and the West were competing with each other to develop still a third power. It was a new and highly dangerous sport.

No, I would not let my trip to the Middle East contribute to this confusion. I was going on my own to collect my own experiences. Crates of books went out ahead of me to various points to serve as demonstration material.

As it turned out, however, this plan fell through completely – in fact, it was a disaster. Most of the crates disappeared without a trace, some fell into the hands of officials already overdeveloped in the developing countries, and battles ensued that were never resolved. Hardly ever did I succeed in getting the crates actually delivered, for there were always important papers missing. Sign language proved to have both an advantageous and disadvantageous side.

[147]

I sent a flurry of letters to Middle Eastern acquaintances and some who were supposed to be friends. At last, I went to a chemist and bought a bulk load of insect repellents, tranquillizers, and something called entero-vioform. What more could happen to me now? My charming assistant, Sabine Eckelberg, promised to keep her fingers crossed twenty-four hours a day.

Overture: The Hilton Hotel in Istanbul, an oasis of luxury in a land of scarcity; the Golden Horn outside, the ruby-red glass bathroom inside, one as breathtaking as the other. It was a splendid base for operations.

I'll attempt to select some of the experiences especially characteristic of each country. *The Animals' Conference* proved that I am no militarist, but I almost became one in Turkey. On Sundays there were more soldiers than civilians to be seen in Istanbul. They were even kneeling on the fabulous carpets in the awesome Blue Mosque, saying their prayers. In Turkey military service lasted three years. These men came out of their villages as illiterates and went straight into army camps. There they learned to read, write, and work with numbers, and afterwards they returned home proudly to teach the new generation.

For many reasons it seemed to be a perfect system. One feature of their service was that the time spent on learning was deducted from the time devoted to military exercises, and thus a lesser chance for the men to develop a passion for soldiering.

What kind of books were available to these soldier-teachers in their barracks? Since the books were in Turkish, and I could not read the language, I could not tell, but by now I had reached the point where I could tell the contents of a book by its smell. These smelled stale, the text-book smell, and that is the same the world over.

I immediately started a campaign in the barracks to 'Learn Foreign Languages Through Children's Books.' I had carried reams of booklists along with me, enough, I thought, for the remotest contingency. I hadn't thought of military bases, though.

[148]

I also carried about with me, by way of ballast, a small, locked case containing all the different pieces of advice people had given me. Here is a sampling:

'The first thing you must do is throw overboard your European sense of superiority. It is so much surplus baggage.'

'Try to speak like a Turk to the Turkish, and like a Persian to the Persians. Always try to worm your way into the other person's skin at any given moment.'

'Never forget, some of mankind's greatest people also were illiterate.'

'Be tolerant of people who don't love children's books as much as you do.'

'Make every effort to learn as much as you can, and teach as little as you can.'

No doubt there was a lot of truth in these words of advice, and in other dicta I received, too. But no doubt also the more sophisticated people were struggling with complexities that blurred their vision as well – especially the Americans. I wondered if anyone realized how thin the line was between humbleness and pride, how easy it was to delude oneself on this point. I was not going to let anybody rob me of my candour, and these were to be *my* experiences. I had met, spoken to, and made friends with people of all races, creeds and levels of education. Of course there were hurdles to be taken, such as an interview I had at the ministry of education in Ankara.

I was talking with Mr Aziz Berker, then head of the library section, with an alert interpreter beside me to translate my English into Turkish, and Mr Berker's Turkish into English. Mr Berker, who was also a highly placed member of the government, had views of his own about libraries and librarians, and he went into great length to detail these views for me. He thought special training for librarians was superfluous and what was really needed were more training courses for teachers. Gradually we began stepping into friendlier waters and made plans for children's libraries.

[149]

All at once, without warning, his face darkened. A torrent of words poured out of his mouth, causing the interpreter to grow pale. Nevertheless, she repeated his words to me.

'Obviously, you consider Turkey as part Asian. I see it now as we are talking. We are Europeans, madam, and I must ask you to remember that.'

I thought back quickly over what had been said. I had provoked the lion. Then I looked him straight in the face, and said, 'I beg your pardon, your excellency. But now I must ask a question of you. Does Europe really mean more to you than Asia? I never would have believed such a thing.'

He returned my gaze, eyes upon eyes. Then he struck his hands together and laughed.

'You are a perfect diplomat, madam. Allow me to congratulate your organization.'

He then served me some sweet, thick Turkish coffee in an eggshell-thin cup, a drink which was worth its weight in gold at that time in Turkey.

During my sojourn in Turkey I also visited, along with a university professor, a little village set in a sandy ravine, where it had lain for hundreds of years. Driving past ancient mud huts in our Thunderbird, we stopped at last in front of a bright new schoolhouse. Immediately we were surrounded by children. The professor acted as my interpreter.

I pulled out a few books and some chocolates from my reserves in the car, and to a little girl, about five years old, who was smiling up at me, said 'Take a handful!' She looked enchanting with a white ribbon that fluttered up and down like a butterfly over her forehead.

'No, thank you,' she said, her face suddenly grave. 'My mother won't allow me to take gifts from strangers.'

'But I'm not a stranger,' I said, and put my arms round her. 'I'm your friend, and I have come here to tell you about children in far-away places, and about the kinds of stories they read.'

[150]

Moments later we were sitting in the warm sand, with children's heads bent low in excited interest over a copy of *The Happy Lion*. Goats, chickens, and a curious mule shared in our fun.

As we bounced back over rutted field roads in our Thunderbird, we happened upon a poignant illustration of the direction aid to developing countries was going. Everywhere we looked we could see late model American farm machinery abandoned in the middle of the fields, gathering rust. Here there were not enough trained personnel, there were no agricultural schools, and there were no repair shops to keep the machinery going. The same thing could happen to us if we weren't careful. It wasn't enough simply to send books out into the world. Schools and libraries must be built at the same time, and scholarships and exchange programmes created. The tractors had trumpeted their call, and we had heard.

Beirut, the Paris of the Middle East, was a city of great diversity in its society, full of tanned Arab children irresistibly charming even when they were beggars. My baksheesh consisted of little picture books and paperback copies of the *Schweizer Judendschriftenwerk* (writings for Swiss children). I was for ever putting them into little outstretched hands, engaging in competition with the American and Soviet authorities who were doing the same thing with millions of comic books, many, unfortunately, of questionable quality.

There were three universities in Beirut, one Lebanese, one American, and one French, a competitive market if one can so describe academic institutions. Anyway, I did my level best to do what I could in such a situation. The chancellors of all three universities promised me their assistance, including their continuing interest in setting up a special training programme for children's librarians.

One morning two Lebanese school headmistresses, dressed in quiet elegance, picked me up in a school bus to show me their schools. Both were girls' schools, one a boarding-school on the English model, and the other an Arab school where students

[151]

qualified for the university. Each had wonderful programmes, modern and traditional at the same time. There were a generous number of classroom libraries, with books in various languages, and there were musical instruments and easels for painting. Almost all the teachers were young and most of them had acquired at least part of their education abroad. I felt a spirit among them that people would normally call Christian, but which have other roots, too, for all of these teachers were devout Moslems.

There was a drive, finally, through beautiful gardens which ended at a barbed wire barrier that defined the no-man's land between Lebanon and the youthful state of Israel; the land of the Bible, rent in two by political misunderstandings. Here it was that I encountered the man-created marvel of the Sputnik, as its brilliant speck moved through the dusky blueness of the sky.

Persia and fairy tales – that was the connection made in my mind as we landed at the Tehran airport. But before I had time to savour this thought, a black-bearded Persian in a white coat advanced upon me holding a hypodermic needle – as always at this time of year there was a smallpox scare in Persia. I managed to shake him off by showing him my health certificate, and I am sure he never imagined the sobering effect he had made upon my gauzy thoughts.

My faith in Persia was restored, however, through an invitation to the house of a prominent Persian, Professor Saba of Tehran University, who also was a delegate to UNESCO. A mere two hours after landing I was standing in the big reception room of his house surrounded by a select group of interesting guests. My feet sank into a carpet whose colours resembled the patina on the roof of a baroque church. Old miniatures, which would be the pride of any museum, shone from their glass cases, and the delicate perfume of an exotic incense filled the air.

In this setting I spoke of the place in the modern world for children's and young people's books, and of the success we had found in having not only the children's classics published in rapid succession in many different countries, but also the best of the new works. I showed picture books whose colour plates had been printed at one time in an enormous run for houses in America, England, France, Italy, and Germany, while the printed text in its various languages and the binding was being handled by the various countries concerned. This method had made reasonable pricing feasible and, most important, it had enabled children all over the world to get their hands on them.

Discussions and private conversations pointed up the problems that were peculiarly true for all countries of the Near East: the uncertain political and economic future, the shocking backwardness and poverty, the illiteracy, and the total lack of planning. Yet anybody could see at the same time that these people had a will to change these conditions, to sincerely catch up with the pace of the century.

It was a bewildering picture. But always and everywhere, for me the centre of that picture was the children.

The scenes of five- and six-year-old Persians working their fine little hands over their looms to earn their daily bread will always haunt me. They were children without the faces of children; they were patient children, resigned to their lots in life, and marked by weariness and poor health. I would offer them my gay little books and they would thank me with a hardly perceptible smile. The beauty of Persian carpets faded before the fact of this child labour. And also before another fact I later learned – the way Persians put a drop of opium on the tongues of newborn babies to calm them down.

I took part in a meeting of the Tehran ministry of education with some delegates from UNESCO, various foundations, and the leading woman in Persian education, Dr Mossaheb. With the reckless abandon known perhaps only by reformers, we ploughed through the entire social and cultural scene of the country in three hours.

Here again, the Sputnik kept me company. The Persians stopped in the streets and craned their necks to get a glimpse of it. Crowds formed, and an elderly man stopped into the middle of one circle and began talking and waving his arms. Was this a political propagandist? Heavens, no! This was merely a good story-teller who had spotted an audience. I listened with pleasure, though I didn't understand a word. One should be aware of one's competition, after all . . .

Now once more I was sitting on a plane – not a wartime Flying Fortress this time, but a jet-speed Caravelle, and not in a diabolical bucket seat, but on foam rubber upholstery. No American colonel in his field gear was asking me about my plans for the next life – 'What would you rather be, a man or a woman?'

As I fastened my seat belt my heart was pounding. It had got me through all kinds of punishment these last years, torn by doubts as it had been, shaken by human needs and human suffering; yet it was constantly being replenished with fresh hope that the idea of international understanding through children's books, which I had tried to pass on to the world, would prevail.

As the land of the Tigris and the Euphrates unfolded itself beneath the wings of the plane, scenes of my postwar experiences crowded my mind. I saw a little girl with a flower waving at me among the ruins of Frankfurt. I saw another child climbing the stairs of the Berlin exhibition hall in the dark winter of 1946, saying to herself, 'Yes, now it is peace!'

I saw a small Negro girl in St Louis, Missouri, paint a Snow White as black 'as the ace of spades', and a little blonde German girl paint a picture of herself with a fish in her stomach. I saw the Young People's U.N., the bright eyes of the girls and boys who wanted to do their part in building a united world.

The International Youth Library and the International Board of Books for Young People were no longer dreams, but established institutions. Even the shortsightedness and narrow-mindedness of bureaucrats could never alter those facts. In many parts of the world children were holding books in their hands and meeting over a bridge of children's books. And all this was only a start. The possibilities were without limit. First the postwar world, now the developing countries – one day there might be a new call, a children's expedition to the moon?

Why not? That was a logical conclusion. For, after all, children have always been interested in the moon. . .

The Book Castle – Dr Barbara Scharioth
Director, International Youth Library

In *Die Kinderbuchbrücke*, Jella Lepman unpretentiously and humorously describes her momentous life's work: the foundation and development of the International Youth Library. Originally written and published in German in 1964, the English translation was published for the first time in Great Britain and the United States in 1969 with the help of the American Library Association. The book opens with Jella Lepman's return to Germany from her British exile in autumn 1945 and closes with the retirement from her work for the library in 1957. Looking back over those twelve years, seventy-year-old Jella Lepman could not have imagined how successful and long-lasting the life of her 'special child', the International Youth Library, was to become.

In 1999, the International Youth Library's fiftieth anniversary celebrations attracted major international interest. Old companions – like Hildegard Hamm-Brücher, who worked with Jella Lepman and her old friend Erich Kästner in the editorial department of the post-war newspaper *Neue Zeitung* during the 1940s; Walter Scherf, Jella Lepman's successor from 1957 to 1982; editor Heidi Oetinger from the publishing house Oetinger; Jella Lepman's children Anne Mortara-Lepman and Guy Lepman; and many, many friends of the Library, amongst them IBBY's president Tayo Shima – came from around the world and were united in deep gratefulness to the founder of the Library.

[155]

All successors have been very well aware of the great challenge and responsibility of guiding this unique library through their times. Since 1983, the International Youth Library has been located in its new domicile in the Blutenburg Castle in the western part of Munich, which dates back to the fifteenth century. Jella Lepman would surely have appreciated today's name, 'Book Castle', both in its literal and figurative senses. The original 8,000 books from twenty-three countries, which were shown at the opening of the International Youth Library in 1949, have grown to a total of 510,000 books in more than 130 languages by the turn of the century.

Since no specialised library can do without secondary literature, by now the stock has expanded to 30,000 volumes, in addition to 40,000 documentaries and 280 current international periodicals on children's literature. Last but not least, the lending library for children provides 20,000 books in sixteen languages, and offers numerous activities for the promotion of reading.

Jella Lepman's dream has come true: The International Youth Library has developed into a centre for specialists of children's and youth literature from around the world. Her vision of international cooperation led to the foundation of the International Board on Books for Young People (IBBY), after the idea of an advisory board for the International Youth Library had failed.

In those early days, Jella Lepman was seeking international acceptance, as well as connections and possibly financial support from foreign countries. As early as December 1949, shortly after the opening of the library in September, she was in contact with UNESCO in Paris to discuss possible ways of cooperating. Those early contacts lay the groundwork for the library's acknowledgement as an 'associated project' in December 1953.

Another step towards international acceptance of the International Youth Library was the three-day conference, 'International Understanding through Children's and Youth Books', which took place from 16–18 November 1951. About 250 participants from eleven countries came to Munich for the event. Jella Lepman gives a detailed account of the conference in the library's annual report and shares her immediate impressions: 'It was the first meeting of the kind which was extensively and exclusively dedicated to this issue. For this reason, it could only be experimental – with all the advantages and disadvantages such experiments entail.'

The conference ended with a meeting in which the participants agreed to found an 'International Curatorium for the Furtherance of the Youth Book'. Richard Bamberger (Austrian Youth Book Club, Vienna) suggested setting up branches of the International Youth Library in each of the member countries. Together, these branches would form the association.

Another proposal proved to be more realistic. The first step was the election of a preliminary Board of Trustees. Represented were Austria, Switzerland, Germany and West Berlin, as well as Norway and Sweden. The Board of Trustees held its first meeting in the rooms of the International Youth Library on the weekend of 3–6 October 1952. This meeting was another step towards IBBY's foundation. This close connection to the International Youth Library, however, was never mentioned later on, not even by Jella Lepman in her *Kinderbuchbrücke*.

Back to the present: Thanks to the generosity of many publishing houses from all over the world, the heart of the Library – its collection of international children's and youth literature – has continued to grow. Since its foundation, the International Youth Library received sample copies free of charge, both for the archive and exhibitions. Nowhere else in the world can such a rich and multilingual stock be found in one place.

Donations of historical books have allowed the International Youth Library to build up a unique collection of about 80,000 volumes, published between 1574 and 1950. The UNESCO Headquarters in Paris donated the collection of the 'Genfer Völkerbund', which can be regarded as an early model collection, to the International Youth Library in 1969. It had been built up from 1928 onwards, and holds 30,000 volumes of children's and youth literature from fifty-eight countries. These books now represent an important part of the Library's historical collection.

Parts of the historical collection (about 20,000 books) are now recorded in an online catalogue and can be consulted via the internet. This new digital technology has been employed at the International Youth Library since the early 1990s, granting access to more than 120,000 titles. In recent years the Library has been given various estates, from internationally renowned writers such as Erich Kästner, Michael Ende, James Krüss, and Otfried Preußler.

The mission and goals of the International Youth Library have not changed much since its foundation. The Library has devoted itself to the promotion of international understanding by collecting, cataloguing, and facilitating communication about children's and youth literature published around the world. The travel exhibition 'Guten Tag, Lieber Feind' (Hello, Dear Enemy), organised in 1998 and first shown in India during the New Delhi IBBY Congress, pays special tribute to these founding ideas. In its updated form, with fifty-five titles from twenty countries in 100 books, the exhibition has travelled very successfully through Japan for two years. It was also shown in Italy, Poland, Slovakia and other European countries. In 2002, it will reach the United States of America.

The annual 'The White Ravens' catalogue, which presents 250 titles from almost fifty countries, equally expresses Jella Lepman's idea of connecting nations. This list has its roots in a 1964 exhibition of new books and is the only compendium of its kind worldwide. For some years now, the annotated titles have also been accessible via the internet.

A virtual walk through the 'Book Castle' is possible anytime on our website, www.ijb.de. And although we are not quite sure whether Jella Lepman would have appreciated this new form of communication, we are convinced that she, a strong woman looking towards the future, would surely have used this new medium to inspire the scene of international children's and youth literature with her great vision.